CHRISTIAN COLLEGE, CHRISTIAN CALLING

CHRISTIAN COLLEGE, CHRISTIAN CALLING

Higher Education in the Service of the Church

Edited by
STEVE WILKENS
PAUL SHRIER
RALPH P. MARTIN

ALTAMIRA
PRESS

A Division of
ROWMAN & LITTLEFIELD PUBLISHERS, INC.
Lanham • New York • Toronto • Oxford

AltaMira Press

A division of Rowman & Littlefield Publishers, Inc.
A wholly owned subsidary of The Rowman & Littlefield Publishing Group, Inc.
4501 Forbes Boulevard, Suite 200
Lanham, MD 20706
www.altamirapress.com

PO Box 317
Oxford
OX2 9RU, UK

British Library Cataloguing in Publication Information Available

Library of Congress Cataloging-in-Publication Data

Christian college, Christian calling : higher education in the service of the
church / edited by Steve Wilkens, Paul Shrier, and Ralph P. Martin.
    p. cm.
    Includes bibliographical references.
    ISBN 0-7591-0934-6 (alk. paper)—ISBN 0-7591-0935-4 (pbk. : alk. paper)
    1. Education (Christian theology) 2. Church colleges. I. Wilkens, Steve, 1955–
II. Shrier, Paul. III. Martin, Ralph P.

    BT738.17.C48 2005
    230'.071'1—dc22   2005010847

Printed in the United States of America

♾™ The paper used in this publication meets the minimum requirements of
American National Standard for Information Sciences—Permanence of Paper for
Printed Library Materials, ANSI/NISO Z39.48–1992.

To our students

CONTENTS

ACKNOWLEDGMENTS

To the Department of Practical Theology at Azusa Pacific University, which gave its vote of confidence to this project when it was only an idea.

To our colleagues in the Division of Religion and Philosophy, who have graciously given of their limited time and considerable skills to make this idea a reality.

To Michael Whyte, provost at Azusa Pacific University, and Diane Guido, vice-provost for undergraduate studies at Azusa Pacific University, who have demonstrated support for this project in intangible and tangible ways.

1

THE NOT-SO-GREAT DIVIDE

Steve Wilkens

It's a story that is replayed time and time again. A group of dedicated Christians decides to start an institution of higher education. After years of praying, planning, and raising money, it becomes a reality. Buildings are constructed, faculty and staff are hired, and the students enroll. Hundreds of Bible schools, universities, and seminaries have originated in this way. Often, and sometimes not too long after the doors open, something odd occurs. The very people who helped give birth to the school become uncomfortable with what happens there. It has been my experience that their discontent usually centers on two different things: Either they believe that the school does not provide students with practical tools to equip them for the "real world," or they determine that students are being taught things the sponsoring group would rather not have propagated, or both. In short, concern has emerged about the orthodoxy and practicality of the education offered, and they may start asking, "What are they teaching at that college, anyway?" This is the beginning of the "not-so-great divide."

The not-so-great divide is what I call the fissure that is common between supporting congregations or denominations and their educational institutions. Far too frequently, these two aspects of Christian ministry view each other with suspicion and even hostility. In the worst cases, bloody battles have occurred. Faculties get "purged" and boards are stacked with the "right people." On the other side of the divide, schools rewrite their charters and drop their denominational connections and sometimes even abandon their Christian identity. In less severe situations, a lingering lack of trust simmers, and an uneasy coexistence takes the place of what should be a close partnership. Fortunately, an uneasy relationship between congregation and academy is not the case everywhere. Many times a good linkage has been forged, and things run smoothly. However, even when an atmosphere of trust and cooperation exists between a school and its constituents, it is sometimes there because the school has substituted indoctrination for education (but we'll talk more about this below).

While the success stories are there, it is clearly not a universal phenomenon. So what goes wrong in those all-too-numerous situations where tension exists? Obviously, this isn't what was planned, and it certainly isn't the way it ought to be. Why does the story of discontent in church-school relationships sound so familiar? More importantly, what do we do to keep it from happening in the first place? How do we find that "body of Christ" ideal where these ministries function harmoniously?

PLENTY OF MEA CULPAS TO GO AROUND

As is often the case in less-than-ideal relationships of any kind, problems result from real faults, as well as from misunderstandings, false perceptions, and poor communications. Most of this book will focus on the second category—the problem of lack of communication and misaligned expectations. However, it will also be helpful to honestly acknowledge some of the real shortcomings that contribute to the not-so-great divide, and educators in Christian institutions certainly deserve plenty of blame for estrangement from the church. For example, quite often in a quest to get top scholars in their disciplines, schools hire professors who do not have a commitment to the Christian faith or the school's theological perspective. In turn, these individuals become involved in future hiring decisions, and over time the theological identity, and even Christian character of a school, can be lost. Many people are surprised to learn that several of the most prominent universities in the United States—Harvard, Princeton, Brown, University of Southern California, and many others—began as Christian institutions but have completely lost any real connection with that heritage. When constituent groups grow concerned about the direction of their institutions, history supports their fears that they *could* be on their way down a slippery slope.

Sometimes, the problem does not go quite as deep as a complete abandonment of the faith, but a gap between the school and the outside Christian world is still there. For example, people who go into post-secondary education often do so because they look at life and faith in a rather cerebral manner. In itself, this is not a problem. However, academics can forget that not everyone is wired in the same way, so they either try to remake the spirituality of their students after their own model or fail to connect with students at all. There can be a tendency to become so absorbed in the academic realm that any meaningful involvement in congregational life is lost. At times, educators have forgotten that their role is not an end in itself, but a means toward a more complete life. Also, each strength comes with its own set of temptations and, to be blunt, academic achievement can lead to arrogance and pride (even though the proper result is just the opposite, in my humble opinion). The sad fact is that academics and their institutions have often failed the church.

While educational institutions should own up to their share of the blame, congregations also have contributed to the tension. Many times, their evaluation of educational institutions has been shaped by second- or third-hand information that is little more than rumor. Anecdotal evidence of some actual misdeed can be taken as the rule, and this is accentuated by the fact that news is usually considered news only when it is bad news. Also, an unfortunate multiplier to the problem of academic arrogance is the insecurity felt by many laypeople and pastors about their own lack of education. Thus, complaints about the people with all that "book learning" can say more about the lack of confidence of the speaker than anything else. It is not infrequently the case that supporting congregations or influential members have very narrow theological agendas and use minor doctrinal points as a litmus test to determine the health of an entire institution.

The problems noted above for both educational institutions and congregations are obviously only a partial list, and it should go without saying that whatever can be done to resolve these issues would go a long way toward improving church-school partnerships. However, my experience as a student in Christian schools, as a church layperson, and as a faculty member also convinces me that much of the disillusionment about educational entities could be removed. This will not happen, however, unless schools do a better job of communicating what they are up to and how they share the same goal as local congregations, even if they go at it in a different manner. This brings us to the specific task of this book.

WHAT ARE THEY UP TO IN THAT RELIGION AND PHILOSOPHY DEPARTMENT?

Obviously, a small book like this cannot look at all the issues that have created rifts between Christian educational bodies and Christian churches. Instead, we will focus our attention on a specific but central aspect of Christian higher education. It is quite often the case that the flashpoint for concern about the academy centers on faculty members in the areas of religion and philosophy. These folks deal most directly with matters of faith and constitute the arm of the school entrusted with carrying on the theological distinctives of the supporting group. Yet, this is also the faculty that is often perceived to be the most problematic by students, supporting denominations and groups, and even the school's own administration. It is not uncommon that even theologically conservative faculties are suspected of "going liberal" by those outside the department. As mentioned above, history tells us that concern about a school's loss of its theological moorings is not an illusion in every case. However, the types of things that get an undergraduate department or seminary labeled as "liberal" may just be a symptom of good educational methods. What can be interpreted as a loss of orthodoxy is quite often nothing more than a lack of communication between the academy and its stakeholders—students, contributors, parents, and others—about what should happen within an educational institution.

Because the religion and philosophy faculty is so often the target of criticism, this book will offer a glimpse at the various disciplines commonly contained in a religion and philosophy undergraduate department or within a seminary structure. The purpose of this is twofold. First, it is often not clear to laypeople what the difference is between the various disciplines contained within such departments (for example, biblical studies and theology), nor is it even evident why certain disciplines are included in a religion or seminary program (for example, philosophy or church history). Second, those outside the academy often do not understand the methods behind instruction in these disciplines, and this leads to suspicion and concern about academic institutions. Therefore, we will ask specialists in each of the disciplines to explain why they teach their subject as they do, ask the sorts of questions they raise, and talk about ideas and thinkers that are often considered outside the mainstream or safe zone. Our hope is that a more focused picture of partnership will emerge in which Christians both outside and within academic institutions work toward a unified goal but do so by using different means. When properly executed, these different means of building up the church can then be viewed as an expression of the different gifts and callings given to each Christian by God.

THE ROOTS OF THE NOT-SO-GREAT DIVIDE

As mentioned above, I'll leave it to the practitioners of the different areas to explain the unique features of their disciplines. However, I want to speak directly about a general issue that is often found at the core of suspicion about Christian higher education—the concern that educational institutions often encourage doubt rather than faith. Here's a scenario that is not uncommon. A group of students shows up for their first Bible class at a Christian college or seminary. Many have attended church all their life; maybe some came to faith a few years earlier in the youth group. Whatever the case, most come with a history of Christian camps, youth group Bible studies, perhaps hundreds of sermons and devotionals heard at church, and a strong desire to grow in their faith. Then, when they open the course syllabus, they find a list of books with unfamiliar titles written by people they have never heard of, a schedule of tests, and due dates for term papers and other assignments, and they are immediately hit with the realization that something is very different here. We're not in church anymore.

As the semester goes along, this awareness intensifies. The students in our hypothetical Bible class fill notebooks with unfamiliar terms, study historical background and literary genre, and are confronted with questions that no one ever asked them before. In addition, they hear ideas that no one ever talked about in their Christian circles, and the tone of the whole endeavor is foreign to anything experienced in their home church or Youth for Christ group. And it's not just in this class, but all across their schedule. They find their profs talking about folks like Darwin, Bultmann, Nietzsche, Freud, and others who had always been represented to them as the "wrong people." Sometimes positive things are even said about them.

It doesn't take an expert in psychology to recognize that students will experience some culture shock. Consciously or not, expectations have been set by their previous experiences about what a Christian education should look like, and none of this classroom stuff fits very closely. When you add to this the fact that some students at Christian schools have heard almost nothing positive about higher education from the pulpit and have frequently been sent off to school with well-intended warnings about the dangers of losing your faith at college, it is a very natural response for them to assume that something is wrong.

Is something wrong at "Christian University/Seminary?" Possibly, but maybe not. The scenario above contains more than a little autobiography. Like many others during their student years, I went through stretches when I wondered whether my college and seminary were guilty of false advertising when they called themselves Christian. There were also times when my classes made me wonder whether I even wanted to remain a Christian. Some of the stuff I believed deeply when I came to school now seemed downright improbable, and my faith underwent some crisis periods. Now, a few more years later than I would like to admit, I'm back as a faculty member in a Christian university. And I'm doing the things my profs did—raising the same questions I confronted as an undergrad and talking about all the "wrong people" (sometimes positively) to students who may wonder whether I'm a Christian, whether their school should be called Christian, or whether they still want to remain a Christian.

I would quickly add that I'm still a Christian and a rather theologically conservative one to boot. So why am I doing the very thing to others that caused so much turmoil in my life? While my colleagues and I know that such methods are often responsible for concerns congregations have about the orthodoxy of Christian educational institutions, the intellectual challenges we throw before our students have a constructive purpose. However, before we can get to the positive intent, we need to make a crucial distinction between questioning and faithlessness.

QUESTIONING AS REPENTANCE

Many are inclined to interpret any form of questioning as doubt. Thus, when questions are posed in the classroom about scripture, doctrine, and deeply held beliefs, it can be viewed as faithlessness toward God and our deeply held traditions (and some do not make a very clear distinction between these two categories). However, there is another way to look at such intellectual examination. Often, it is not lack of faith in God or a theological tradition that we find behind questions, but a lack of faith in ourselves and a natural response to our fallenness. While faith-based institutions affirm the trustworthiness and completeness of God's truth, there is plenty of evidence that we should not have the same level of confidence about the accuracy and adequacy of our own *ideas about* God's truth. It would also be helpful to remember that whatever theological tradition you value arose as a result of someone questioning previously held belief systems. In a similar manner, the type of prodding that comes in a college setting is ideally viewed as a confession of our own need for intellectual repentance and renewal.

Any Christian activity should involve a hefty dose of repentance and desire for renewal. In our private prayer, we search the recently past moments of our life for those areas where we have fallen short of God's will, seek forgiveness, and ask God's grace in a new start. And, we might note, we cannot do this without examining and questioning our actions and interactions. Ideally, the academic setting involves these same twin concerns for repentance and renewal, although it will manifest itself differently in such a setting. Through critical thought we examine our life, traditions, presuppositions, and beliefs. Sometimes we find that they are the best expressions of truth among the options we have examined; at other times we find areas where our current ideas need revision. In either case, we have gained something. This is why questions are such a key part of the educational process. If we do not inspect our beliefs, we run the risk of deifying our own opinions or our theological traditions, which is always a dangerous proposition. Any decent statement of faith will have a clear statement about the universality of human sin and limitation, and the testing and questioning included in education is the natural response to this tenet.

MAKING FAITH OUR OWN

Concerns may still linger for many about whether a constant testing of beliefs and ideas is ultimately destructive. Again, the answer is not a simple yes or no. If you watch two people taking something apart, an automobile engine, for example, the observation that an engine is being dismantled does not give you the entire story. One person may disassemble an engine out of anger, boredom, ignorance, or perverse destructiveness with no intent to ever reassemble the pieces. Another, however, may have a keen desire to understand how the various engine components fit together in order to know how the entire system functions. By "dissecting" the motor thoughtfully, insight is gained into internal processes that cannot otherwise be seen and understood. The intelligent mechanic may even find ways to make the whole thing run better. There is in any kind of renewal process a certain amount of destruction that occurs. This is not the goal, however. The disassembling and destruction is only the prelude to the constructive work of understanding and improving. This type of activity is inherently messy. Even when we have the best intentions, valuable pieces can get misplaced, and what initially seemed like a brilliant idea may prove to have an unforeseen flaw in hindsight. We can get frustrated by the whole process and leave everything in pieces on the workbench. Learning our theology is subject to the same types of dangers as discovering the secrets of the internal combustion engine.

The ideal in Christian higher education is that the novice should be under the supervision of a more experienced "mechanic" who can offer guidance when the novice is up against the wall. Knowing when and how long to allow a beginner to make mistakes and struggle and when to step in and suggest resolutions is part of the messiness for the teacher, and this knowledge is certainly more art than science. Despite the untidiness of the process, it seems to embody two principles behind in any solid educational process. First, real learning necessarily involves personal involvement and experimentation. Without these two ingredients, what could be education degenerates into indoctrination. When involvement and experimentation are dropped into the mix, however, we get the volatile elements that make people queasy. Experimentation, as we have noted above, inevitably involves mistakes. When involvement is required, the stakes skyrocket. We are not just talking about errors involving friendships, automobile purchases, or career choices. We are dealing with a person's life—their worldview, the eternal, spiritual aspect of their life, their faith, the whole ball of wax. This awareness is something that keeps a good professor awake at night.

This leads to the second important principle. Education must be rooted in the experience of the educator. This does not include just the professor's commitment to the content of the course, but also an awareness of what happens as a result of the educational process. Many of the contributors to this book remember serious faith struggles from their own student days when they wondered whether their prayers and pleas for help bounced back off the dingy acoustical tiles on the dorm room ceiling or if a benevolent and merciful God heard them. Many of the certainties they brought with them to college no longer looked bulletproof. Like Jacob, they experienced all-night wrestling matches that left them gasping for air. When they came out on the other end of these struggles, they were different. They would also tell you they are better people—and better Christians—for it.

Of course, there are no guarantees that everyone will turn out the better for the experience. That is what concerns a school's supporters as they watch students endure this process of testing and struggle. So wouldn't it be better to play it safe and not confuse people with questions and different views? Some educational institutions do go in this direction, and it can help constituents feel more comfortable with what happens in their school. However, in addition to other concerns that I will not address here, the thing that haunts many Christian educators about the "safe" approach is what I call "the phone call that never comes."

THE PHONE CALL THAT NEVER COMES

Bible schools, Christian universities, and seminaries have an important element in common. They are tuition-driven institutions. If they annoy their constituencies too much, they run the risk of going out of business. This makes Christian schools much more sensitive to customer criticism than your average state-funded university. Given this situation, when a student's parent or pastor calls and asks, "What are you teaching at that college, anyway?" administrators tend to pay attention. Then the call goes downstairs to the department chair and finally to the professor alleged to be guilty of garbage spewing. If done correctly, there is something very good about this process. Every school needs to be accountable, and some professors need to be called into question. At other times, the problem isn't actually intellectual junk, but a misunderstanding about what an educational institution should be doing (not to mention unfounded rumors or half-truths).

As you can guess, administrators and professors do not like to get such calls, and it is cause for alarm when they come. However, good Christian educators balance trepidation about constituent phone calls against a fear of "the phone call that never comes." Here's the situation. A student sails through school without ever seriously reflecting on her beliefs, either because those beliefs did not face the types of challenges intended to test and build faith in the classroom (the prof's or school's fault) or because the student ignored the challenges that were presented (the student's error). Diploma in hand, the student goes out into the world and, somewhere along the line, gets nailed by some crisis that she lacks the resources to deal with. As a result, she abandons Christianity. It happens, and it happens far too often. When it occurs, however, no one ever calls the school to ask why the professors did not challenge this student's ideas in ways that would have helped her prepare for inevitable crises of life. It's "the phone call that never comes."

In short, one of the reasons teachers do the things they do is that the "safe" approach turns out not to be so safe in the long run. For the short term, it is easier to avoid controversial topics, ideas, thinkers, and questions. Students, administrators, and the school's constituency are often much happier when this occurs. Moreover, when things do fall apart later in life, no one calls them to account for what they did not do. The basic flaw in the so-called safe route is that it is better described as indoctrination than education. Indoctrination is imposed on you. Education occurs only when a belief system has been internalized through the processes of experiment and involvement described above. Thus, when the indoctrinated person loses her faith, it is a bit of a misnomer. It was never *her* faith in the first place, but was something borrowed from someone else. When one has not struggled to gain something, it does not take much to give it up.

CHRISTIAN HIGHER EDUCATION AND
THE QUESTION OF PRACTICALITY

Obviously, most of what precedes this deals with concerns about the orthodoxy of the academy; but when we talk about the type of education that prepares a student for life beyond school, we have moved toward the second concern about Christian institutions—the question of practicality. We have already acknowledged that the "ivory tower" criticism has a measure of validity. Schools can forget that students will go on to do something other than take classes, and to this extent they fail the test of practicality. However, I will also argue that certain things that many consider impractical in a student's learning process are in reality some of the most useful aspects of their education.

A phrase I hear tossed around frequently is "that's only a theory." No one ever comes right out and says it, but this phrase is intended to seal an argument and signal victory for the person who opposes the so-called "theory." It also assumes a common belief that theory is the polar opposite of what is practical and that what works in practice constitutes truth. Both of these assumptions are on pretty thin ice. First, we do not just do things. We have reasons behind our actions. What we do (practice) is the result of a set of beliefs (theory) about what is good, useful, or true. In other words, we may not be conscious of the theories that inform our actions, but they are always in the background. Therefore, if you want to do the right things, a good theory is a necessary guide toward what should be done. The second assumption—that what works is equal to what is true—depends on our beliefs (theory again) about how we determine whether or not something works. Getting high may "work" briefly in helping me forget my problems, but it will not "work" in solving them. Building your life around a lucrative job may "work" toward providing a *comfortable* life, but fail miserably as a way to obtain a *good* life. We sort out which definition of "works" is the correct one in terms of our theories about what is important in life. This is why one of my profs used to state that there was nothing more practical than a good theory. If that is true, then it is not a strike against education when it pays attention to theoretical matters. In fact, I have no hesitation is saying that an education that does not include a theoretical component is completely impractical (and also not an education).

While I want to make a strong case for the theoretical side of the educational process, I would hasten to add that educators should give attention to how theory applies to the concrete realities of everyday life. It is possible to have a good theoretical grasp of the world, but very little ability to put it to use in navigating the rapids of life. For this reason, we have asked the authors of each chapter to go beyond a simple description of what is involved in learning the content of their discipline. They are also charged with the task of explaining how it can be used to help students grasp their vocation, or calling.

Because the idea of vocation has different meanings in various contexts, we want to be clear about how we will use the term. In secular culture (and too often in the church), vocation is defined in terms of a job, what you get paid for. On the other hand, in Christian groups, vocation is often used to refer to a full-time professional ministry. Neither of these definitions, however, gets at the more traditional understanding of vocation. The word itself comes from a term that means "calling." The broader Christian sense of the word refers to God's call to live faithfully in whatever endeavor God has placed before us, employing whatever talents and gifts he has granted us. Thus, all Christians have a vocation, or calling. How we live out our specific calling will differ from one Christian to the next, however.

With this definition in place, you will quickly recognize that a Christian view of education and vocation will include much more than outlining nifty strategies for functioning as an elementary school teacher, marketing manager, or whatever job you may have. It is even broader than helping students put together a great career, even though it will include such things. Instead, since God's calling encompasses the whole of our life—our relationships, our gifts, and our aspirations—when we speak of the practicality of the various disciplines, we will think far beyond the paycheck. While God's interest in our lives includes what we do between 9 a.m. and 5 p.m., it extends to more than that. The goal of the following chapters, then, is to provide some clues about the practical use of the theological and philosophical disciplines in fulfilling God's calling for an abundant life. The chapter on practical theology toward the end will provide a model that shows how the different areas of study have contributed toward a more complete understanding our vocation. This model will also suggest ways (without any pretense of being the only way) of applying the truths of faith to our actual experiences in life.

CONCLUDING COMMENTS

We want to acknowledge up front that all the authors write from the perspective of full-time faculty in a Christian university. This may give the impression that this is just another case of academics trying to justify themselves to skeptical outsiders. However, while these authors are academics, they are not *just* academics. The majority of them have been students in a Christian university or seminary or both. They have seen the story from the student side of things, and their first-hand experiences come back again and again as they help their current students work through their own questions and struggles. Each also brings the congregational perspective. We have led Bible studies, taught Sunday school classes, changed diapers in the nursery program, endured endless committee meetings, sponsored youth trips, and carted numerous casseroles to church potlucks. The majority of the authors are also ordained clergy, some with a long history of service in local church ministry before coming into the teaching profession. The point is that each author writes out of love for the academy, the congregation, and the student and is heavily invested in all three worlds. We also write out of recognition that the tension that so often exists between the congregation and the academy does not have to be there. Instead of suspicion, our desire is that the ministries of Christian higher education are in sync with those of the local congregation.

Most of the solid marriages I've observed have two features. First, both partners have very similar values and goals. Second, the partners have personalities that differ but are complementary. Each brings to the marriage something the other does not have, and these differences contribute to a wholeness that cannot be found in the partners individually. Perhaps this provides a useful template for what should be a good marriage between congregation and academy. Both should be shaped and directed by kingdom of God values and goals but should also recognize the unique and distinct roles, gifts, and methods in our kingdom work. Good Christian educational institutions do not simply mirror the activities of a healthy congregation. Instead, schools bring together people with unique and necessary gifts to provide an aspect of ministry that complements the activities of congregation ministries. However, the differences in method should never obscure the all-important goal shared by both—the full maturity of the Christian. We can achieve this unified goal without demanding uniformity in our approaches. In fact, Paul's metaphor of the body of Christ indicates that the vitality of the church is stunted if we insist on uniformity. A healthy unity exists only where the full diversity of gifts, talents, and functions are present and healthy. We hope this book provides a small step toward transforming the not-so-great divide between congregation and academy into a great marriage of two vital centers of Christian ministry.

2

BEING GOOD: AN INVITATION
TO ETHICAL THINKING

Daniel Speak

Somewhere between my freshman and sophomore years of high school, I committed myself to Christ. Of course, like most folks, I had very little idea what becoming a disciple of Jesus would entail. All I knew was that I was supposed to learn from him how to live my life. Very shortly after this initial commitment, I began to study the Bible with my youth pastor and some friends. Our church was located directly across the street from my high school, so a group of us would cross the street during our lunch break for greasy fries (what other kind are there?), prayer, and Bible study. Most of the topics of these sessions are now lost from my memory. But there was one session that I can still vividly recall.

We had been looking at Jesus' Sermon on the Mount when we came to his startling teaching that if a man looks at a woman lustfully he has, in essence, already committed adultery with her in his heart. Amidst the roiling of my adolescent hormones, these verses immediately caught my attention. The teaching struck me as radical, perhaps impossible to comply with, or maybe just plain wrong (I mean, isn't it just obvious that there's a world of difference between thinking about having sex with someone and actually doing it?). Over time, with the encouragement of my youth pastor, I came to see the brilliance—and liveability—of Jesus' teaching on this topic. This was a crucial step in my spiritual development. This step was crucial, in part, because apprentices of Jesus must learn how to gain a kind of control over their thoughts, especially when it comes to their sexuality. More important than this particular recognition, however, was the more general realization dawning upon me that discipleship made a radical demand. It required that I come to see the entire moral world as Jesus did. It would not be enough to make the right statements, claim orthodox beliefs, or even act in good ways most of the time. My commitment to Christ involved me in a revolutionary way of seeing the world and living in it. I could no longer live accidentally, thoughtlessly, or by default (as I had for the years leading up to my conversion). In giving my life to Jesus, I was agreeing never to run from the question, "How should one live?" and always to respond to it in light of my master's wisdom.

The ancient Greek philosopher Socrates thought that the question about how we should live was the most important of them all. Even if you don't want to go this far, you'll have to admit that it is certainly *among* the most important. Our attempts to answer it in a systematic and philosophical way constitute the academic discipline we typically refer to as "ethics." In what follows, I'm going to try to motivate you to take the study of ethics seriously as a disciple of Jesus and to dispel some common misconceptions that might keep you from engaging its topics. Among other things, I believe you will be able to see that studying ethics can contribute to your understanding of the distinctive ways God has called you into his work in the world. My main strategy will simply be to explain why, as a Christian scholar, I teach and conduct research in philosophical ethics. My hope is that in sharing some of my passion and concern for the issues, you will find yourself not only with greater understanding, but also with some newfound appreciation for and curiosity about the philosophical foundations of morality.

So, why do I do what I do? Why do I teach, think, and write about ethics? I had better be honest up front and just confess that one of the reasons is that I enjoy it. Frankly, this stuff fascinates me to no end. Everywhere I turn, the moral world calls out to me for explanation or confrontation. The questions simply won't go away. What is right and wrong in a certain situation? What *makes* right actions right? Does it depend on God in some way? What way could this be? Are we always obligated to tell the truth? Can one obligation ever conflict with another, so that I can't help but violate one of them? What makes a person truly good? What is really worth going after? Is pleasure the only thing? How about happiness? And what is the difference between these two? Are there ethical truths that do not depend on what people think or feel about them? And the list goes on. These questions get under my skin and into my head inescapably. I want to think and read more about them, try to formulate answers to them, chop them up into small enough pieces to chew, swallow, and digest.

You may be like me in this respect. But you also may not be. And even if you are, you may be wondering what the study of ethics is good for. In particular, you may be wondering how it is good for the Christian community. There is much to say here (especially about what it means to be "good for" something). But let me try to put my response in terms of calling. I believe the study of ethics can serve the Christian community by helping to clarify and develop the concept of vocation. It certainly has done this for me. And it has done this in two particular ways. First, it has increased my understanding of how I should live in response to God's love. Second, it has contributed to an intellectual defense of the Christian community's basic convictions and commitments. Since space is limited, I am going to focus my attention on the way my *understanding* has been increased. Perhaps after reflecting on this discussion you will find yourself interested in the role philosophical ethics could play in a *defense* of Christian principles. In that case, you will have a motive for further study. (See how I'm trying to trick you into taking ethics classes? Sneaky, aren't I?) As I develop these ideas in the following paragraphs, I am convinced that, if you permit it, your reflections on ethics can enhance your awareness of and commitment to your own distinctive calling.

Before moving forward, I should add that studying ethics is not a substitute for living as Jesus calls us to live. My hope, of course, is that ethical reflection can help us live better. But ethical reflection and ethical living are two different things. There are many people who have engaged in very little by way of philosophical deliberation about morality but who are nevertheless excellent examples of Christ-like living. Similarly, there is no doubt that some of the greatest ethical minds have done very little to translate their thinking into sincere and disciplined behavior. A person can live well without studying ethics, and a person can live poorly while studying ethics. Philosophers sometimes put this point by saying that intellectual reflection on ethics seems to be neither necessary nor sufficient for a good life. This is a warning to all (including myself) not to fall into the trap of confusing academic pursuit of truth with its honest expression in action. I do not believe, as some have insisted, that these two are opposed to each other. But I do believe that we should have their difference clearly before our minds. Otherwise, we fall prey to two related mistakes. The first is being satisfied with empty, ivory tower abstraction in the absence of real living. The second is passionate action without clear principle and reason. The antidote to both of these mistakes is to take on the mind, heart, and will of Jesus. In him we find the perfect marriage of systematic thought and authentic commitment. Only in him, then, will our study of ethics bear the fruit I have suggested we can anticipate.

I should also make explicit at this point what I trust you may have inferred already. Christianity *is not the same thing as* ethics. Ethical theory, as I am considering it here, is the branch of philosophy concerned with what principles people have reason to live by that are discoverable by the kind of rational reflection available to any open mind. Of course, Christianity has much to say about which principles to adopt and which to reject. And Jesus is, without question, one of the most penetrating ethical thinkers in history (even from the perspective of those who do not grant him any special religious status). But none of this means that Christianity *just is* living according to the best principles accessible to unaided human reason. Christianity is, instead, much broader than this. This is because it involves questions not just about what to do but also about what to believe, how to interpret scripture, how (if at all) to construct an overarching picture of God. Furthermore, Christianity does not claim to limit its boundaries to those truths that can be discovered by reason alone. Rather, it proclaims quite openly that much of what matters most must simply be received through revelation of some sort.

So, studying ethics (along with the other disciplines you are reading about in this book) is only one component of the larger project of gaining understanding. And gaining understanding is only one component of living the Christian life. Even if gaining this understanding is, in some ways, indispensable to Christianity, we will do well not to conflate them.

Now, let's think about this potential fruit in a little more detail. I have suggested that studying ethics can increase our understanding of what it means to live as Jesus would have us live. How? Well, whatever particular calling you have received (or will receive), it surely involves being a good person in general. Unfortunately, most people have almost no idea what being a "good" person actually involves. We don't really understand goodness. In light of this, consider the apostle Peter's insistence that we "make every effort to add to [our] faith goodness; and to goodness, knowledge." (2 Peter 1:5). He seems to be challenging us not simply to *be* good, but also to *know* what goodness is. And this is consistent with Jesus' entire manner of life and teaching. Jesus is never satisfied with mindless obedience, but always presses his disciples to penetrate more deeply into their master's own mind and heart to see his reasons and motivations. Of course, on some occasions, we will have to proceed by blind obedience because, for one reason or another, we aren't presently able to grasp Christ's underlying reasoning. But this cannot be the standard pattern for a maturing student of Jesus, just as it cannot be the pattern for a maturing child. As my son (now ten years old) continues to develop, it is my joy to help him see, more and more, the rationale behind the rules he has been expected to follow. This is Christ's joy as well, and we should not rob him of it. After all, the goal of our discipleship is not simply to conform our outward lives to him, but to come to think, feel, reason, and then act like him. This means, among other things, that we will need to think and reason about goodness as he does.

ARISTOTLE AND GOODNESS

The nature of goodness is a central concern of philosophical ethics. A proper study of the great ethical traditions can, then, illuminate the Christian mind and sharpen our thinking about a concept crucial to our life in Christ. It can help us add knowledge to our goodness. (I assume, always, that this study is undertaken by a person devoted to and lovingly immersed in the biblical narrative.)

Two particular philosophers, with very different perspectives on morality, have been enormously helpful in shaping my own views about being good. Let's start with Aristotle, Plato's most famous student. To get us going, take a minute to think about someone whom you admire . . . and make it someone you actually know. Once you have the person in mind, make a short list of the things you admire about this person. Have you got your list now? I'm going to make a prediction. Your list is dominated not by particular actions that the person has done, but instead by traits of character—things like commitment to friends, discipline, perseverance, courage, compassion, patience, love, etc. Am I right? Do you have any particular actions on your list? You might have something like "always treats people with respect." But notice that this isn't a particular action. Rather, it is a *habit* or *disposition* to perform particular actions. What does this show? Well, at least this: that we admire people not primarily for what they do, but for who they are. Of course, who a person is will be expressed in what she does. But you cannot tell what kind of person someone is by seeing her action on one occasion.

The modern perspective on ethics has been focused on right actions. And right actions are surely important. We blame people for doing the wrong thing on particular occasions, and we praise them for getting things right. Punishment and reward also seem to be connected with particular actions. But for the ancients, and especially for Aristotle, right actions depend on right character rather than the other way around. Admiration is morally more important than praise and blame.

One implication of this approach to ethics is that models or exemplars become absolutely necessary and central. We need people to admire and imitate. Becoming a good person requires that we have good people to watch and after whom to model our lives. For Aristotle, when a person asks, "What should I do in this case?" the answer is to be found in what the truly good person would do in those circumstances. If you don't know any truly good people, then it will be exceedingly difficult to reach the right conclusion. Most of us know at least a few people whom we can admire and imitate, so we aren't in terrible shape. But as Christians we have an enormous advantage. Why? Because our faith is rooted in the life of Jesus, a flawless example of a life lived well.

Aristotle still has more to teach us. We need examples of good people, indeed. But to become good ourselves it is not enough merely to watch such people, or read stories about them, or develop theories about what all good people share in common. Imitation is absolutely necessary. So, in Aristotle's view, you become good only by *practice*. That is, you have to do what the good person does. Knowing all about good people will not make you good. This is because goodness is not a feature of your thinking alone, but of your entire personality. Perhaps some of your thinking can be changed by simple transfer of information (though I'm even suspicious of this), but the rest of you needs to be transformed by the hard work of imitation.

This begins to bring out another aspect of Aristotle's moral thought that can be of great service to our understanding of the Christian call to goodness. Good people perform the right actions by *habit*. This is to say that you haven't really become good until you have developed a natural disposition to do what is right. When we imitate a good person, what we are trying to do is become someone with the same internal patterns. If I do what love demands on a particular occasion but fail to do so on the next three occasions, then I am not loving. I'm still in the process of becoming loving. Not until my good actions come naturally and regularly have I developed the particular moral excellence. In a sense, then, the good person is someone who is no longer *trying* to be good, but who simply has goodness flow out of her by nature.

KANT ON GOODNESS

So, Aristotle gives us a picture of the moral life that is focused on character and habits. Immanuel Kant, the eighteenth-century German philosopher, places his moral emphasis elsewhere. He begins his most famous ethical treatise by insisting that only a good will is truly good. I take it that what he means by a good will is a proper *intention*. And this might lead you to wonder if Kant could have been right. After all, haven't we all been told that "the road to hell is paved with good intentions"? People often want to do the right thing but simply are not able to bring themselves to do it. Why would someone think this kind of intention could be the deepest kind of good possible when it might not be enough actually to bring about the intended result?

Here's what I think Kant had in mind. Take any quality of a person that you are inclined to think of as good—intelligence, perseverance, honesty, whatever. If any of these qualities is in the service of a person with bad motives, then the goodness of the quality will actually make the bad person worse. Think about it. Isn't a smart criminal worse than a dumb one? If a person is a foul racist, then won't his honesty be a bad thing? A violent dictator possessed of perseverance will only be able to be more effective in his tyrannical pursuits. So, Kant concludes that intelligence, perseverance, honesty, and just about every other good trait are really only good under the right conditions. These qualities aren't unconditionally good. They aren't "good without qualification."

But a good intention, a good motive, a good will can never be put into the service of evil. Can it fall short of its goal because of weakness? Sure. But in the service of a bad will, the other traits become bad when they succeed. By contrast, a good will converts all the other traits that serve it into excellences. If an evil person came to have a good will, then that person would cease to be evil. If an evil person came to have courage, then that person would be even worse. This, I think, is what is moving Kant to make his initial claim. Some goods are conditional. Only a good will is not.

But we do not yet know what Kant thinks a good intention or will amounts to. What would it mean to have a good will? Well, he argues that a person has a good will when he attempts to do what is right simply because it is right. In Kant, then, we find one of the clearest accounts in history of an ethics based on *duty*. If I am a good person, then what should move me to act is the fact that a certain course of action is what the moral law demands. Notice that there are three possible responses to what duty requires. First, you might perform the action that duty demands in a certain case (say, telling the truth) precisely because you know that it is what duty demands. Second, you might perform the action that duty demands, but for some other reason (for example, because it will keep you out of trouble). Third, you might fail to do what duty demands altogether. Of course, in the third case you are bad and are worthy of moral blame. But in Kant's view, only the first you is good and worthy of praise. The second you is neither good nor bad. Others are probably glad that you have done what duty calls for, but since you didn't do it for the right reason, their appropriate response to you would be moral indifference. What you have done is simply not in the realm of morality. It is, instead, like choosing the bean burrito over the chicken soft taco. We just don't care about it from a moral standpoint.

This brings out how important motives are for Kant. And it is worth reflecting on this aspect of his thought because of how illuminating it can be for our thinking as Christians. For Kant, in agreement with Jesus, what moves you is at least as important as what you actually do. Suppose I have never committed adultery (as it turns out, you needn't merely suppose this—it is true, too). You might be inclined to think that I deserve some minimal moral recognition for my fidelity. Of course, you think that this is exactly what was expected of me, but there is still a sense in which you might be tempted to think me morally praiseworthy. But now further suppose that I tell you I have wanted to commit adultery for years. In fact, I have made a number of plans to violate my wedding vows, but either the plans have fallen through or I have chickened out for fear of getting caught and losing my job. I assume, now, that you will have very little temptation to consider me worthy of any moral praise. What seems to explain this is that the moral world is considerably deeper than our outward behaviors. Our intentions are crucial to our goodness. On this score, Kant must be right. If you and I are satisfied with conforming our outward actions to the moral rules, then we are just legalists of another sort than the pharisees, no more in possession of goodness than those who thought they could please God by keeping the law.

Kant was also deeply troubled by the way that many people determine what they should do by considering what would *result* from the action. This approach is usually called "consequentialism," because the rightness of actions depends on the consequences. What Kant seemed to be concerned about was the way that being focused solely on the results of an action could blind you to more important moral matters. For example, if you are only considering what will result from your action, then you might ignore the fact that you made a promise to someone in the past. Most importantly, Kant claimed that our fundamental moral commitment should be to treat every person with respect. In particular, he noted that respecting a person means never simply using her for your own purposes.

Now, he realized that we all use each other from time to time. The person behind the counter at the fast food joint is useful to you when you want your burger. You use your professors to get an education. I assume you are using me right now (if not to learn, then at least to get done with some tedious assignment). But in all of these cases it is possible for you also to recognize that the other person has her own plans, aspirations, life projects. You can use another person in these ways as long as you, at the same time, respect her life projects that have nothing to do with you. Kant makes this point by saying that we ought never to treat people as means only but always at the same time as "ends in themselves." If I manipulate, coerce, or trick you into doing what I want you to do, then I violate this moral rule. By ignoring the fact that you might have your own plans to attend to, and by not giving you a real choice about joining my project, I fail to treat you as an end in yourself. I have used you as a mere means to my ends.

Think about this radical view. What lies behind it is Kant's intuition that a person is of incalculable worth. A person's value is, again, unconditional. This means, for example, that you cannot exchange one person for another. In fact, you cannot exchange one person for any number of other persons. Each person is of infinite value. The value is, so to speak, "off the charts." So, two people aren't more valuable than one. Infinity is infinity. Infinity added to infinity doesn't equal anything more than infinity. Not only, then, is one person as valuable as two, but one person is as valuable as five billion. Talk about the sanctity of human life!

This allows us to see the fundamental danger of consequentialist moral thinking, from Kant's point of view. If the rightness and wrongness of our actions depends solely on the results of what we do, then we will inevitably treat people as mere means and not as ends in themselves. This is because it is sometimes true that the best overall consequences can come from treating people as mere means to some truly remarkable or seemingly necessary end. Sometimes it will be better overall to trade a few lives for many, many others. As you can see, this kind of thinking isn't simply in minimal tension with Kant. It is its absolute opposite. In Kant's view, almost nothing could be morally worse than to make such a trade with lives, as if a person were a car or a piece of furniture. Kant's thinking on this point, as with all radical views, has some disturbing implications that I won't take the space to discuss (I'll leave these implications for you to think about . . . as homework, so to speak), but his basic worry seems compelling. A results-oriented approach to ethics will inevitably involve reducing people to "stuff" that can be exchanged for other "stuff." Something must be wrong, then, with such an approach. The good person cannot be concerned only with what happens as a result of his actions.

TAKING STOCK

Let's take stock of what we have picked up from these two giants of moral thought. I have emphasized Aristotle's focus on moral models, his insistence that goodness is a result of practice, and his suggestion that goodness is principally demonstrated in habits rather than in particular actions. From Kant, I have noted his emphasis on the central role of motives or intentions, his commitment to a nonconsequentialist approach, and his idea that persons are of incomparable worth. I trust that it is more or less clear how these features of Aristotle and Kant's views can be translated into a distinctively Christian approach. What emerges, I think, it a picture of the good person that matches quite deeply the one we get from Jesus as we watch his life and take his teaching seriously. From my perspective, Aristotle and Kant (and many others besides) help us to understand Jesus and his call upon our lives. Of course, some moral philosophers have more to offer us as Christians than others. Not all ethical theorists are as worthy of our attention as Aristotle and Kant, and some might be outright useless to us. But even those most opposed to Christian morality (like Nietzsche, for example) can show us fascinating and important things about how to live and be. This is, in part, what fires me up to study these complex ideas and unique figures.

Now, let's think just a little more about the idea of "calling" or vocation. I don't know what God has called you to in particular. Maybe you are yet to sense such a call. Maybe, even, you are suspicious about the very idea of receiving some particular calling. In any case, you surely will agree with this: Your calling from God will not be simply to be or do a particular thing. That is, your vocation will not be to be a businessperson, or a teacher, or a missionary. Rather, it will be to be a *good* businessperson, or a *good* teacher, or a *good* missionary. Part of being a good whatever involves possessing the relevant skills and training for competence in the activity. I'm not a good baseball player if I can't field my position or hit reasonably well. Similarly, lacking any sense of rhythm will insure that I won't be a good musician. Let's call this the competence side of goodness.

What we have been seeing in our reflections on ethics is that the competence side of goodness is not all there is. From a Christian perspective there is also a moral side of goodness, a side that has to do not with one's skill or training, but with one's character and motives. You will not have been faithful to your calling to be, say, a good pastor if you are enormously successful at the tasks of ministry but lack the inner transformation urged on us by the great moral thinkers. The same, of course, is true about being a good journalist, politician, coach, parent, salesperson, or what have you.

A quick example: A close friend of mine is an attorney. Indeed, I believe that he is a *good* attorney. From the standpoint of competence, this means that he understands the subtleties of the law, has developed the oratorical skills necessary to present a compelling argument in court, possesses the critical thinking, reasoning, and writing skills necessary for producing forceful briefs, etc. But Jeremy's goodness goes beyond competence. That is, he has come to understand his calling as more than a set of tasks to be performed and skills to be developed. Instead, Jeremy is motivated by a broader and deeper set of concerns about the nature of the law, justice, fairness, and the like. As a result, he aims, (unlike many of his colleagues) to treat each of his clients as a real person and not as a mere source of income. Their cases are not simply problems to be solved but components of a person's life that are the cause of much heartache and frustration with which he can sympathize. He is not unique in billing his clients honestly, but likely *is* somewhat unique in doing so not because he might get caught if he lies, but instead because this is what honesty demands. Rather than ask, "What practices will produce the greatest amount of personal wealth?" Jeremy consistently asks "What needs am I in a position to respond to?" and "What traits of character is God pressing me to develop?" For this reason, he frequently takes pro bono cases (cases for which he does not receive any payment because the clients are too financially strapped to be able to afford payment). Jeremy is a picture for us of what it means to be not only a *competent* attorney but also a *morally good* one. And this picture of moral goodness can be repainted in any area of vocation.

With Jesus as our ultimate model, then, we have been able to learn from Aristotle and Kant about the nature of this moral goodness. And this has been only the slimmest introduction to philosophical ethics. The tradition has so much more to offer us. As you continue to explore your calling, I recommend further exploration of this ethical tradition. In my own life, I have been deeply challenged not to rest content with what might be called "accidental" morality. Indeed, it seems to me that apprentices of Jesus simply cannot do so. We all need to be prodded to allow the transforming work of Christ to penetrate further into our character. Ethical theory can function as just such a prod. In conclusion, then, I urge you not to allow the competence side of goodness to replace or override the importance of the moral side. Satisfying your calling will require you to attend to both.

3

"PHI-*LOST*-OPHY" OR "LOVE OF WISDOM"?

John Culp

Sometimes philosophy appears to be a major contributor to the split between the college and the church in the "not-so-great divide." After all, some philosophers spend their lives denying that God exists and take great pleasure in making fun of people who believe in God. Should Christians therefore avoid philosophy, or should they trust God as they study philosophy? Paul says that height and depth cannot separate us from God. In fact, he says that nothing at all can separate us from God's love (Romans 8:39), and we should assume that philosophy is included in that. "But," someone might object, "even though philosophy doesn't have to keep you from God, it could; so why take the chance?" Your mother probably warned you against walking across the street without looking both ways because you might get hurt. You didn't refuse to look both ways just to see if you could get across the street. So why study philosophy just to see if God can protect your faith? Is philosophy valuable enough to make it worth studying even if it may challenge your faith? A lot of preachers, theologians, saints, and even philosophers have thought philosophy is worth the risk. To show why philosophy is worth studying, I want to talk about what philosophy is and how studying philosophy is helpful for Christians even if sometimes it does taste like medicine or feels like running a marathon.

THE NATURE OF PHILOSOPHY

What is philosophy? Is it something so deep and misleading that many people get lost, or were the Greeks right in calling it the love of wisdom? A student once said that philosophy was what men who have been dead for four hundred years do. While I immediately thought of all these people who had been in heaven for four hundred years working on their philosophy, the student meant that philosophy is something completely detached from what is happening today. Sometimes, teachers make philosophy sound that way because they talk about the ideas of earlier philosophers without showing how those ideas are important to us today. But often those early ideas can help us today. The *Matrix* movies excited a lot of people because they recognized the possibility that computer technology could destroy our ordinary ideas about reality. However, five hundred years earlier, Descartes, a French philosopher, had already grappled compellingly with the question of whether our perceptions matched reality. His thoughts on this matter may help us even more than *The Matrix* as we deal with the computer-generated virtual reality of today. No one needs to reinvent the wheel, and it's just plain stupid not to learn from others' mistakes and insights. Thus, the ideas that come through someone's experiences of reality, even from a long time ago, can benefit our own thinking.

You have some ideas, ideas about what you will do after you finish reading this chapter. Your ideas may be about what you really want to do and what you actually will do. Does that mean you are a philosopher? To some extent, everyone "does philosophy" if they ever think about what is real or true and what to do because of what is real and true. But saying everyone is a philosopher doesn't help much in showing what philosophy is. We need some understanding of how philosophy relates to other areas of thinking and studying. Philosophy is the effort to think very broadly about reality, to think about all of reality. Other areas of study tackle a specific aspect of reality. As an example, biology tries to understand the functioning of living organisms. Biologists develop ideas about living organisms within specific systems and environments and defend their ideas about those living organisms. Philosophy broadens the scope of investigation. When philosophers look at biology, they investigate the assumptions biologists bring to their study, the forms of knowledge they accept and the kinds of knowledge that biologists can and cannot provide to our broadest view of reality. While biology may do a great job in helping us understand a species of herring within a particular ecosystem, it may not be very useful for getting at subjects like God, morality, or questions about freedom of the will. Thus, philosophers will combine the findings of biology with ideas from other disciplines to try to fill out the picture and clarify our concepts, recognizing the arguments that people have given for those ideas and checking them out to see if they are adequate. Philosophy even pushes the question back to examine how we determine what is actually true.

WHY BOTHER WITH PHILOSOPHY?

This relatively simple explanation of philosophy raises the question of why we should bother studying philosophy. Trying to understand something as specific as language is hard enough; why try to think more broadly? After all, knowing Chinese will help you get lunch in Beijing. You don't need to understand all the different ways that people use language to get lunch. Suppose philosophy does talk about God. Why study philosophy to learn about God? Why not stick with theology or the Bible? Isn't that sufficient for a Christian?

Even though philosophy may be difficult and may seem impractical, there are important reasons to study philosophy. The first reason is to develop your ability to think abstractly. When Lucky, my Labrador retriever, chews the end off the plunger, I think a number of thoughts ranging from "What a stupid dog" to "I have to buy a new plunger." Sometimes our thinking deals with the mess the dog made. At other times we think about how and why the dog likes to chew on things and then make sure he's outside before we leave. The first type of thinking works with physical objects that we can see and smell. But when I think about characteristics of Lucky and his tendency to chew on everything, I'm not thinking only about physical objects. Thinking about relationships, characteristics, reasons, and the past or future requires memory, imagination, and the ability to relate ideas to each other. Most people get enough practice thinking about physical objects from the time that they were born that they develop their abilities to think concretely. But thinking about abstractions, characteristics of concrete objects, is a different game.

All of us can improve our abstract thinking by practice, and philosophy gives you that practice. You will compare concepts to see how they are similar and different and examine whether those similarities and differences are important. After all, dogs and tables both have four legs, but you don't feed your table. By practicing the art of abstract thinking in your philosophy class, you will also begin to recognize different ways of organizing what you know and how you came to know those things. Knowing your mother loves you is different from knowing which factors led to the Civil War. Philosophy will also help you understand which way of learning works with which type of knowledge. You can't experience the Civil War even if you take part in Civil War reenactments. But you can experience your mother's love even though it may seem like she has a strange way of showing her love at times.

Philosophy can be a challenge because it makes you study people who think differently from you. However, examining different ways of thinking is another good reason to study philosophy. Some philosophers will have ideas that you would never think of in a hundred years, and they may say things that you know are wrong. Some of them will help you understand how they decided something was wrong in a way that is different from how you knew that it was wrong. For example, you may have rejected materialism since it seemed to leave no room for God, but some philosophers might alert you to the challenges to materialism from the direction of ethics. Examining a variety of ideas and ways of thinking will help you appreciate and use new, different, and (sometimes) better ideas. That appreciation will enable you to defend different perspectives because you will have some experience with the ideas involved in other ways of thinking. This skill will also allow you to anticipate how a person who disagrees would respond to your ideas.

Anticipating an opponent's arguments may be satisfying, but more importantly, it can help you recognize the basic principles behind your disagreement. You can't stand the old peoples' hymns that they always want to sing in church. The older folks always complain about the newer songs that really mean something to you. How do we get to the basic principle behind this tension? Could it be that you are both worshipping God? Or are there songs that you like that don't worship God but just make you feel good? Studying different perspectives in philosophy will allow you to better analyze the issue at hand and give you more ways to respond. You don't have to disagree automatically, but you also don't just have to accept what everyone tells you. Philosophical training provides the means to understand different perspectives and draw value from them.

In addition to helping you think abstractly and deal with different perspectives, your courses in philosophy (you do want to take more than one now, don't you?) will enable you to evaluate systems of ideas. People today often talk about the importance of worldviews such as a modern worldview, a scientific worldview, a postmodern worldview, a Christian worldview, or a Muslim worldview. Worldviews, as systems of ideas, are very difficult to identify and evaluate because you can't point to them (which brings us back to the relevance of abstract thinking). Yet they are very important because the way we think about something affects what we do with it. For example, you may like the lock on the door to your room or house because it helps you protect your stuff from people who might just take it. But if you aren't worried about someone taking your stuff, you may never lock your door. If the door is never locked, it is essentially the same thing as not having a lock on the door. Even a simple example like this demonstrates that what you think about the people around you (an important part of your worldview) has a clear influence on how you will live. Since worldviews are important for what you do in your life, you will want to have the best worldview possible. You can't get the best worldview possible just by paying more money than anyone else does. You also don't want to just take anyone's word about what is the best worldview, because that can be as dangerous as thinking someone's dream means you should invest all of your money in a hamburger stand in India where people don't eat cows.

To identify the best worldview possible, you will need to do the hard work of thinking about worldviews and evaluating them. You will need to develop some criteria for what is a good worldview and what is not a good worldview. You will have to find alternative ways of thinking about things if a worldview doesn't do a very good job of bringing meaning to your life. Philosophy helps you collect worldview resources by offering explanations for why things are the way they are. That will help you understand what counts as evidence and what doesn't. For example, Plato taught that this life is never all that it can or should be. But Plato also had some ideas about how we can know what this life should be. Aristotle, Plato's most famous student, had different ideas about how we can know the purpose of life. A contemporary scientist might disagree with both Plato and Aristotle on how things are and what life should be. Because philosophy has introduced you to different levels of knowledge, you may agree that the modern scientist might provide the best information about the physical world, but that will not necessarily mean that our scientist will offer better views on life's meaning than Plato or Aristotle. Using your own experiences and ideas, you can then think more clearly about the nature and the meaning of life, and can create and test alternative conceptual systems.

Your understanding of reality, your worldview, has a lot to do with what you decide to do in life. Are individual people important? Is there really a God who cares about me? What is the purpose for my existence? All of those questions have answers that will direct you in college and after college. Philosophy by itself won't give you the best set of answers for your life. You are going to have to work on that. One of my friends says that his goal in life is to have a goal in life. He's joking, but he's also right to some extent. You are alive and changing. It is important that those changes have some direction to them. But the direction may change from time to time. How do you know when and how to change direction? The task of living can be made more manageable and successful with the help of philosophy because it gives you experience in dealing with different ways of thinking about life. Those ways of thinking can help you come to conclusions that will give you direction.

Your philosophy class can also help you practically by helping you think in new ways in your job. Learning to think abstractly is crucial for all of life and especially for your contribution to the people around you through the job you do. Sometimes the toughest part of a job is knowing how to act as a Christian in our work situations. How will a Christian nurse or salesperson interact differently with those she serves? Being able to find and compare ideas about how Christians serve God through their work will make you a better Christian in your job.

Another difficult part of most jobs is figuring out what to do next. "What to do next" doesn't just refer to the next five minutes or the next week but involves anticipating what the job will require when the situation changes. It may be that you discover a whole new group of people in the area where you are a social worker. How are you going to relate to this group of people? What problems are they facing that you can help with? What is your responsibility for them? All of these kinds of questions are about what to do next. Because you have improved your ability to think about what isn't right in front of you, you will be better prepared to handle what to do next.

Finally, you will discover that philosophy becomes enjoyable as you work with it. Enjoyment isn't the most important reason for doing something, but it does make life more satisfying. Have you ever heard an idea that helped you answer a question or solve a problem? Do you remember that sense of satisfaction in finally having an answer? Have you ever found a new approach to a problem that looked like it might pay off? Philosophy often brings that kind of excitement as you study ideas. Sometimes philosophy will bring you the insight that clicks and makes your existence worthwhile or helps you understand God's relation to the world. All these experiences in philosophy bring joy and are just plain fun.

GOD, WORSHIP, AND PHILOSOPHY

Since it makes a big difference in peoples' lives, the existence and nature of God is one of the most important questions about reality. Philosophers, poets, preachers, gurus, and all kinds of people talk about God and their ideas about who God is. And yet philosophy is not just talking about God. While many philosophers go to church and worship God, that is different from what they do as philosophers. One way of describing the difference is to say that it is the difference between studying how to be a nurse and being a nurse. Philosophers study ideas about God to evaluate their adequacy.

Some philosophers conclude that the ideas about God are important for reality; others conclude that ideas about God mislead people. The arguments that philosophers on either side of this issue develop to convince other people they are right are important for anyone who is trying to understand what God is (or isn't) all about. However, praying to God doesn't require arguments. Worshipping God is a way of relating to God. Living for God is acting on the basis of ideas about God in a way that affects people's ideas about God.

People talk about God in church, in philosophy classes, and in late-night arguments. When philosophers talk about God, they have to explain ideas and give reasons to support them. When people tell what God has done in their life, they share an experience they have had. Being a Christian and part of God's church is about living for God. This requires ideas about God, but it does not require arguing to support a particular idea about God. A person who lives for God may give reasons why they live that way as part of telling someone else about God, but they don't have to do that in order to live for God. Philosophers have to defend their thinking, while believers do not.

The difference between philosophy and living the Christian faith raises a question about the relationship between them. Some people might be willing to say that philosophy has something to say in certain specialized cases where it is helpful to be able to think broadly. However, they would go on to say that there is no role for philosophy in the church. The popular argument often follows a general pattern, even if it is never stated out loud.

1. Philosophy studies people who not only don't believe in God but also argues against believing in God.
2. Studying philosophers who don't believe in God will destroy students' faith.
3. Therefore studying philosophy will destroy faith in God.

Sometimes the problem is identified as the problem of pride in that philosophers trust only in their own reason and think that they know more than God. In any case, those who follow this line of thought might argue that, while there is some practical use in taking courses in biology and English, Christians should avoid philosophy courses like the plagues of atheism and pride.

The church's relationship to philosophy is a complex and sometimes contradictory one. Both sides have, at times, refused to have anything to do with the other. Some philosophers believe the church keeps them from the truth. Sometimes the church identifies philosophy with the devil. The interesting thing is that church leaders frequently have used philosophical ideas (often unconsciously) to make their case that the church should not be contaminated by philosophy. At other times, the church has relied heavily upon philosophical thought and concepts from non-Christians. Christian apologetics makes extensive use of philosophical ideas and arguments.

Philosophy and faith, theological explanations of beliefs, and spirituality do differ from each other. Sometimes the differences are important disagreements about what is true and real. Those cannot be resolved easily and sometimes should not be resolved at all. At other times, the differences are matters of language and goals. Even if you didn't know the title of the Bible or a philosophy book, you would recognize that they were different types of writing. The Bible talks about God and what God is doing in the lives of nations and people. A philosophy book may or may not talk about God. If it does talk about God, it comes at the question from the perspective of how people think about God rather than from the angle of what God is doing. Philosophy uses a specialized, specific language to develop careful distinctions, while the church uses its own specific type of language to make a point or apply an understanding of God. A second difference between philosophy and the church is that they have different goals. Philosophers seek to understand reality and to express that understanding in a precise way. The church's aim has a different trajectory and puts its focus on showing people God's love for them and calling them to accept God's love. Nevertheless, differences in language or goal need not be complete and radical. Both philosophy and the church talk about God and seek to know the truth. Thus, there are significant intersections between philosophy and the church despite differences. An analogy might be two different activities that are both classified as games (e.g., chess and baseball), but operate under separate sets of rules.

WHAT PHILOSOPHY CAN DO FOR CHRISTIANS

Perhaps the most helpful approach to the relationship between the church and philosophy is to ask what philosophy can do for the church. Knowing philosophy can make a contribution to the church in a variety of ways. Although philosophy is often identified with doubt and questioning, these are very much part of a life of faith. In possibly the earliest example of doubt in the church, Jesus didn't ridicule Thomas for being suspicious about the accounts of the resurrection but gave him evidence to answer his questions. Moreover, the fact that Jesus pronounces a blessing on future followers who will believe without seeing seems to indicate that he knows that such belief does not come easily. Interestingly, the greatest faith is demonstrated when the greatest doubts are present. Asking questions about Christianity requires the faith to believe that answers to those questions can be found. If there aren't any answers, we soon stop asking questions. Otherwise, we would eventually stop asking "Why?" to everything our parents say. Philosophy, by asking lots of questions, and by asking the really foundational questions, helps us find responses that reflect thoughtfulness, not just simple feel-good answers.

Philosophy can help us find careful and clear answers to our questions about who God is and what God wants us to do by opening our minds to new ways of thinking. This, in turn, can help us express God's love to the contemporary world more effectively. Philosophy makes us receptive to more adequate ways of thinking with its warnings against becoming too attached to limited and incomplete answers. Thus, when the government makes money available for churches to help homeless people, refusing to be involved in anything the government does may keep a church from loving its neighbors. Observing that philosophical ideas have changed can help us recognize that our ideas also need to change sometimes. Philosophy also helps us consider the long-terms results of ideas. For example, what happens to a local church if it begins to depend upon government money to help it love its neighbors? Philosophers have experience in evaluating how ideas influence what people do over a long period of time and can help the church understand the long-term impact of different ways of thinking.

Sometimes it is not our ideas that need to be changed but the way we put them into practice. Philosophy helps distinguish between basic principles and ways of applying those principles. For example, love for others is a basic principle. In the 1800s in the United States, starting orphanages was an important way of showing love, and many denominations and local churches did this. Today, however, there is little need for orphanages as a transition from one family to another family. In fact, most of those orphanages no longer exist as orphanages. Instead, some now function as social agencies seeking to help families deal with the stresses that cause family disintegration. Others have moved into providing bridges between government agencies and churches for foster care of children. Philosophy can help people remember that the goal is to show love, not to run an orphanage.

Philosophy can also help the church communicate effectively. While philosophy does not come up with the good news of God's love for us, it can help us communicate the news about that love in Christ Jesus to people. Sometimes the stories about Jesus just sound strange to people today. Because philosophy helps us identify what is really important and what isn't, we can find ways in which people today seek God, even though they might not understand that Jesus Christ is the son of God. Paul demonstrated this use of philosophy in talking to the people in Athens (Acts 17:16–34). He noticed that they worshipped many gods and that their philosophers had talked about the desire for contact with the ultimate source of all reality. Paul used their philosophers and practices to explain Jesus Christ's resurrection as the fulfillment of what they sought.

Sometimes the news of God's love does not seem relevant in our ordinary experiences. Philosophy can help us integrate our faith into everyday experiences in ways that show how the Gospel makes sense. For example, C. S. Lewis drew on philosophical ideas to write *Miracles*, a book that has helped many understand how we can use modern science for our cell phones while also believing the miracle of Jesus' death and resurrection.

Philosophy can help us discover manifestations of the Gospel in places that we never expected to find them. Contemporary philosopher Merold Westphal has written a book of Lenten meditations showing how modern atheists such as Marx and Freud might help the church understand more clearly our need for Christ. Westphal argues that our concern for our own interests blinds us to the reality of God's love and the necessity of God's action in Christ to show us our need of God. Although God made Christ known in the New Testament, the New Testament also talks about how people sought their own interests and didn't recognize God's action of love in Christ. Westphal argues that Marx, Freud, and other secular philosophers also recognize our tendency to understand reality in ways that fit our own interests, and they also see a type of blindness that results from our narrow self-interest. Thus, Westphal makes the point that Christians can find common ground with even the most secular thinkers concerning the basic human problem and the outcomes that result from it, although they express this in a vocabulary different from that of the New Testament. However, God is not limited to our ways of thinking about how God ought to show love and, Westphal concludes, God can use Marx and Freud as well as the New Testament to help us analyze our situation. Philosophy, in its search for the truth about reality, discovers that truth in places where most of us might not look. In finding God's love in "all the wrong places," philosophy helps the church experience the breadth of God's love and find new ways to communicate that love to people who might not recognize the news of God's love in the ordinary places.

WHAT TO EXPECT FROM A PHILOSOPHY CLASS

If you have never had a course in philosophy, knowing something about what happens in philosophy courses may help you get more out of your first philosophy course. "Questions, questions, questions" gives a good summary of what happens in philosophy classes. Questions asked by the professor, questions raised by the readings that you aren't even sure how to ask, questions you begin to ask yourself. But don't let all the questions scare you. The truth is important enough to ask questions about. The fact that truth is important also means that people will have different ideas about what the truth is. As you involve yourself in this search for truth, it is wise to get help from others by asking questions and carefully considering the ideas of those who have already thought carefully about these questions.

Where there are questions, arguments can't be far behind. Philosophy classes are filled with arguments between people trying to discover the truth, and that makes philosophy complex. The truth ought to be defensible, so you will need to give reasons for what you understand to be true. We also have a right to expect reasons from others who defend a different view of truth. Offering a coherent argument for a position is the responsibility for anyone who makes a truth claim. None of us is wise enough to say, "This is true because I say it is."

All this questioning and arguing sounds like a tension-filled existence, and there is often a significant element of tension in well-considered ideas. There are no simple answers that settle all the arguments. Often, we like simple answers because they are simple. In fact, one of the criteria for theories in physics is simplicity. But theories also have to account for all of the data, and that makes for complexity and tension. So in a philosophy class, you will recognize the differences between ideas about truth and the importance of those differences. You probably can pass a lot of philosophy courses by just memorizing names and ideas. But getting your money's worth out of any philosophy course will involve you in questioning, arguing, and living with tension in order to find the truth. You can do it, and only you can do it for yourself.

PHILOSOPHY AND CHRISTIAN CALLING

While I have given some brief examples throughout the chapter about the nature of philosophy, what it can and cannot do, and its use for Christians, it will be helpful to draw some of the ideas into a specific example. After all, God encourages us to become involved in what God is doing in the world, and I have argued that philosophy can enable you to be more helpful in supporting God's purposes for specific situations. So let us suppose that God has drawn you to be involved in a local church that has a deep desire to provide real help to people who are desperately ill. There isn't any money in the church budget for such an expensive endeavor, but you discover that the government has money available for the type of things your church could do. Should your church seek this type of funding for a good purpose?

One of the first things philosophy can help us do is to sort through the principles. We may be convinced that it is consistent with God's nature and will that congregations get involved in ministry to the sick. Government also has an interest in providing such care, but its reasons for doing so may be different. Philosophy can help us think through whether the aims of church and government in providing this care are consistent enough that a good partnership will be formed. This will raise questions about such things as human nature (Where does our physical well-being and care for the sick fit with the God's plan for humanity?) and ethics (Can our congregation accept money with government restrictions and still maintain the integrity of the church's mission?).

Philosophy can also help us think through the practical aspects of such a partnership and may offer alternatives we have not yet considered. Should our church set up a separate structure or participate in a similar ministry to the sick that is already in place? If a government agency has money earmarked for a particular type of work with the sick, do we need to narrow our original vision for such a ministry to a specific type of care? Alternatively, we might ask whether such restrictions might take us too far afield from what the church had identified as its ministry.

Philosophy can push us further in our thinking than we might otherwise go. As our congregation thinks through its ministry to those who are sick and whether or not cooperation with the government will be fruitful, we may begin to wonder about the more fundamental issue of why people are sick rather than focusing on just the symptoms of a problem. Saddleback Church in California has a wonderful program to feed all the homeless in their county for one month. But what happens to those homeless people after that month? Is there anything that can be done to help people find homes? What are the causes of homelessness in that particular county? Could our church do something about those causes? What are our ultimate aims in helping people overcome homelessness and the problems that lead to it? Those types of questions need to be asked, and philosophy can help you ask and think through these questions. If homelessness is an obstacle for those who seek to live a meaningful life, how we go about helping people find housing requires a philosophy about what gives life meaning.

In cases like these, as well as any other real life situation, philosophy will help you identify your purposes and consider how they fit into a broader worldview, think in new and exciting ways about what could be done, explain why God's love guides your mission in ways that others will understand, and open you to unexpected new insights that God can give you. Admittedly, all this question asking and evaluation is hard work. However, if our aim is to experience the fullness that God desires for our life, it also seems to be necessary work.

4

HERMENEUTICS: WHY DO WE HAVE TO INTERPRET SCRIPTURE ANYWAY?

Gerald H. Wilson

It always seems to happen at the beginning of the school year. A sincere first-year student will ask the question I have been waiting for since the previous fall. "So, why do we have to interpret scripture anyway? My Bible seems pretty clear to me! I just read it and trust the Holy Spirit to guide me to the right understanding. What's all this fuss about interpretation?" Students who ask this type of question are often serious, if not yet fully mature, Christians. Many have a long history of church attendance and Bible reading. They affirm the truth and authority of scripture and understand it to be the word of God—although they may not always have a clear sense of the consequences of those affirmations. The questions they raise about interpretation are not bad questions to ask and in fact offer one of the best teaching moments any college professor could want. What is the rationale behind this course? Why are we doing what the syllabus says we are going to do?

So, why *do* we interpret scripture? In what follows, I will discuss a number of factors that come into play whenever we sit down to read the Bible. These factors are necessary consequences of the very nature of scripture itself, and they force us to acknowledge that reading the Bible *always*, *necessarily* involves interpreting what we read; it is never as simple as just reading the meaning off the surface of the text. By the end, I hope you will have a better understanding of why a course on interpreting the Bible is an important part of the curriculum of a program of Biblical studies and why all Christians need to learn and practice principles of interpretation.

THE LINGUISTIC FACTOR

The first factor related to the interpretation of scripture has to do with the realization that the scripture in which God chooses to reveal himself is thoroughly enmeshed in the realm of human language. We call the Bible the *word of God*, and *words* are the linguistic building blocks of meaning. In reality, these combinations of sounds are *symbols* intended to point the reader to the concepts, ideas, or objects that are the real subject of conversation. The combination of the letters *c-h-a-i-r* means nothing in itself but has significance by an agreement among persons to relate this word to a concept that can describe a wide range of objects employed for sitting. We might rearrange these letters differently or use an entirely different set of letters altogether. The word is not the object but only a symbol for a concept of which the particular object is just a single example.

There is, therefore, an inherent ambiguity in the very nature of language; what we say is only a symbol for what we think or see or feel, and that symbol may conjure up different visions of its object for speaker and hearer. If I say *chair*, for example, you may think of that worn, leather, Barcalounger of which you are so fond, while others may think of a stiff, uncomfortable, straight-backed chair at their dining table. This inherent ambiguity of language is particularly acute when we seek to speak of things divine in the very limited words of human language. Look for example at the rather tortured language employed in Ezekiel's description of God in the opening chapter of his book. *What* is he talking about!?

Language is inherently ambiguous and notoriously imprecise. For this reason we must use many words and even develop special vocabularies when precision is of the utmost importance. Philosophical discussions and legal documents are just two examples of contexts in which exact language is considered necessary since truth (or our very lives) may depend upon it. Nevertheless, despite our best attempts to pile up words to make our meaning precise, there always remains a gap between our statements and the reality to which they refer. Ambiguity always leaves an opening for misunderstanding—it is just the nature of language. Thus, one reason we must interpret our Bible when we read it is that the language in which its message is couched is inherently ambiguous and requires more than superficial attention.

THE LITERARY FACTOR

Related to the first but distinct from it is the second factor we encounter. The Bible is *written literature*, not oral spoken language. When the decision was made to write down the oral traditions that became our biblical literature, a new layer of issues was added to the inherent ambiguities of language. What were once sounds are now converted into letters—another layer of symbols separating the reader from the concepts or images in the mind of the original transmitters of traditions. In addition, writing down dynamic spoken traditions has the effect of fixing the tradition in one particular form. My grandfather was a master storyteller. He used to regale us children with tales of his boyhood travels from Tennessee to Texas in a buckboard and the myriad of experiences he had along the way. The basic character of his stories always remained the same, but the nuances shifted and changed—expanding and contracting in response to the particular performance setting and audience response. Once oral narratives are fixed in writing, however, this flexibility is lost, and the narrative has but a single form to be read.

We also lose much more than flexibility in this process. The written tradition becomes a decidedly *one-sided* conversation. No longer do we have access to important clues of meaning and nuance. We cannot see the speaker's facial expressions or hear the tone and volume of her voice. Gestures and body language are entirely absent, and we are no longer able to ask for further clarification or explanation. Imagine a distant traveler (in a time before cell phones!) who receives a written communication from her beloved. How eagerly the recipient will read "between the lines" to interpret the disembodied voice in the absence of these important unwritten clues to meaning!

All reading requires interpretation. Because of the ambiguity of the underlying language; because of the added symbolic nature of the written form; because of the absence of unwritten cues of tone, volume, gesture, and body language, misinterpretation is always possible, and a variety of understandings is probable. For this reason a range of literary tools is necessary for the interpretation of written language. These tools include, but are not limited to, knowledge of the meanings and nuances of specific words, knowledge of grammar and syntax, understanding the use and function of symbolic language, familiarity with different types of writing, literary structures and techniques, and characteristics of literary genres.

While we can assume some basic competence among our students in vocabulary, grammar, and syntax of translations of the scriptures into their native languages, we must provide assistance and guidance in their acquisition of skill to understand the specific forms of symbolic language, literary structures, and written genres of the biblical literature. Prophetic oracles are very different from historical narratives. Legal statements must be approached differently than lament psalms or proverbs. The techniques of Hebrew poetry are distinct from those of traditional Western poetry, and Apocalyptic literature must be read differently from prophecy or the love poetry of the Song of Songs. For this reason we must interpret our Bible because it is made up of an almost bewildering array of distinctive types of written language that must be encountered with full knowledge of their characteristics and techniques for full understanding.

THE TRANSLATIONAL FACTOR

Not only has God chosen to reveal himself and his purposes in human language fixed in a written literature, but he has done so in a particular set of languages (Hebrew, Aramaic, and Greek) that are no longer spoken in their ancient form and are not understood by the majority of Christian believers. This fact involves the serious student of the Bible in the effects of the third factor of biblical interpretation we must consider. Most of us encounter the Bible in various translations into our native tongues. As anyone knows who has ever struggled to acquire a second language, translation is always an inexact process. Other than some basic nouns of relationship (mother, dad, brother, sister, etc.), there are very few direct one-to-one correspondences between any two languages. As a result, translation always involves loss. Often a single Hebrew word exhibits a variety of nuances that would have to be translated by several words in English. A translator must choose the most appropriate or likely correspondence in the particular context under consideration. This means the reader of the translation has lost the possibility to decide for herself among the nuances of the original word. Even within the same language, translation of passages may differ considerably.

Translation into another language may also introduce ambiguities that are not present in the original language. When the Greek words *philia* (love between friends), *eros* (erotic love), and *agape* (selfless love) are all translated with the English word "love," the specificity of the original language is muddied by all the nuances associated with "love" in our world. We "love" our grandmothers, candy, the color purple, rock music, friends, our spouses, and our children in different ways. Whereas the Greek is much more specific, the translation ends up far more ambiguous to those unable to consult the original languages.

Add to these instances of translational ambiguity the fact that our understanding of ancient biblical Hebrew and Greek is only imperfect at best, and you have a recipe for confusion. Most translations include at the foot of their pages notes indicating difficulties of translation. The notes to the book of Job are littered with references such as: "Meaning of the Hebrew uncertain"; "Hebrew word unknown"; "Hebrew obscure"; "Probable reading"; "Hebrew unintelligible." The Hebrew of this book is notoriously difficult and unclear, but since translators are not employed to write gibberish, the translated text reads straightforwardly as if there were no barriers to understanding.

Translations are always interpretations of the original. Thus translators must constantly clarify obscure passages, speculate about unknown words and difficult constructions, and choose between multiple nuances. Because translators are human, they tend to decide these questions of translation in accord with their own theological beliefs and traditions. Thus translations normally share a theological drift that is distinctive: conservative, middle of the road, liberal; protestant, Roman Catholic, Jewish, Orthodox. To open oneself to a variety of possibilities and nuances, the serious student of the Bible will read a number of translations from a broad theological spectrum to avoid becoming myopically limited to a single theological bias.

The translational factor has implications for our understanding of the level at which scripture's authority resides. If the truth or message of scripture is translatable, it must reside at the level of the message rather than the individual words in the original languages. If not, then only those who master Hebrew, Aramaic, and Greek can fully access the truth of scripture, and then only imperfectly. The rest of us are limited to the ambiguous approximation offered in translations. Rather than a wooden, word-for-word translation, modern translational theory (on which all our contemporary versions are based) assumes a *dynamic equivalency* approach in which the message of the text at the level of sentences is distilled and then converted into the target language. This tends to downplay the importance of specific words and emphasizes instead the meaning communicated by those words. Already then, the texts we employ in our native languages are interpretations of the original texts.

THE HISTORICAL FACTOR

Thus far we have noted a series of factors that recognize the essentially verbal and literary nature of scripture as written language with all the inherent ambiguities of that form of communication. Now we need to look at another set of factors that are not so much concerned with the surface *meaning* of the text as its *significance*. The first of these involves us in the realization that all texts—whether fictional or factual, poetry or prose, history, legal, worship, or romance—are produced in a particular historical context and are influenced by that setting. Histories of the Civil War written in the North and South immediately following that conflict reflect different understandings of the issues (slavery, rights of states versus those of the federal government) that lay in the background. And twenty-first century historians of that struggle have a different perception formed by almost a century and half of reflection on the war and its consequences. The differences between these accounts are a reflection of this factor: Our understanding of history is influenced by the context from which we view it.

Sometimes this historical connection is readily apparent, as in the books of Kings where evidence of historical concern is clear (dates, correlations between kings and events in different countries, chronologies, etc.), and the narrator overtly critiques kings and events on a theological basis. But even where such evidence of historical concern is lacking (as in the book of Job or many of the psalms and proverbs), we can be certain that those who were behind the production of each book were part of a particular historical context that shaped their concerns and affected the shaping of their materials.

Even in the clearly historical books, we must acknowledge at least *two* levels of historical relevance within each book: the historical context *described* in the narratives of the book, and the historical setting *to which the narrative speaks*. Take the books of Samuel and Kings in the Old Testament. These books describe events that stretch from approximately 1050 B.C. until the destruction of Jerusalem in 587 B.C. Our best estimation, however, is that these books came to their final form as canonical literature around 200 B.C. to inform and challenge those living in exile. So, to fully understand the intended message of these books we must ask what the active issues were among those for whom they were written.

These historical books are not just a video camera that records uninterpreted events, but highly selective, theologically concerned documents that explain, convict, convince, persuade, challenge, and change those who read them. Once we recount all the events recorded in scripture, we have only just begun. We must then seek to understand *why* these few selected events are reported as they are. What message do they seek to convey and to whom? This quest will involve us in an attempt to reconstruct the original historical setting of the readers of these texts as clues to the message they intend to teach. The proclamations of the prophets can better be understood if we study the historical and social settings to which they speak. Many allusions to historical events, persons, institutions, and attitudes can only be fully understood through deeper historical research.

However, some texts resist all our attempts to haul them into the light of historical understanding. Sometimes this is simply because our historical knowledge is too limited. In other cases, documents are just not very concerned with matters of history. Many of the psalms were preserved and transmitted precisely because their setting was general enough to encourage reuse and adaptation to many different circumstances. The Song of Songs remains romantic love poetry regardless of who the speakers are thought to be. The origins of the individual proverbs are shrouded in mystery, but their advice and guidance is still available to the reader.

THE CULTURAL FACTOR

As historical ignorance can lead to misinterpretation of scripture, so lack of cultural knowledge can prevent full understanding as well. The Bible, Old and New Testaments, was written in and to alien cultures. Without such cultural understanding, we are constantly in danger of importing our own ideas where they do not apply. One good example of this is the constant translation of the Hebrew word *nefesh* as "soul." Our understanding of the soul has been influenced by Greek philosophical thinking in which an immaterial soul exists within our material body during life, but separates at death to continue to exist eternally. The ancient Hebrews had no such concept! For them, the *nefesh* was the physical being that is animated by the spirit of God. At death, God's spirit returned to him and the *nefesh* became a corpse. References to "my *nefesh*" in the Old Testament (Psalm 103:1) are equivalent to "myself" or "my inmost being/truest self" rather than some eternal soul with a life of its own.

To understand our Bibles, then, we must navigate unfamiliar terrain and learn the significance of some new cultural practices, like sacrifices, the levirate marriage, nazirite vows, and curses that are really expected to accomplish their destructive intent. We will encounter institutions based on a cultural ideology unlike our own: kingship, priesthood, temple worship, prophecy, wisdom. And in some instances we will have to make judgments concerning whether pronouncements are so culturally conditioned that they are no longer binding on faithful followers of God today. Take for example the commandments in Deuteronomy prohibiting women from wearing "men's" clothing (22:5) or from wearing clothing woven of wool and linen together (22:11). Making decisions about these sorts of cultural issues in scripture involves us in acts of interpretation— whether we realize it or not.

THE CONTEXTUAL FACTOR

We have looked thus far at the inherent ambiguity of language and literature and the need to compensate for our lack of historical and cultural familiarity with the setting of biblical texts. Now we need to consider another group of factors that kick in once we start to carry out our interpretive task of reading scripture. First, because scripture is a literary construct of ideas and images, context is absolutely necessary for right interpretation. It is possible to prove almost anything by pasting passages of scripture together out of context. As the old saying goes, "Even Satan knows how to quote scripture!" We actually see him in action as he tempts Jesus in the wilderness by quoting snatches of Old Testament scripture in order to dissuade Jesus from following God's path of suffering and death. Jesus' response to the first of these temptations is particularly instructive. When Satan quotes Deuteronomy 8:3 to encourage him to use divine power to turn stones into bread for his personal benefit, Jesus replies: "Man does not live by bread alone, but by every word that comes from the mouth of God" (Matthew 4:4). Jesus is rebuking Satan for taking scripture out of context!

To interpret rightly we must consider each passage in its appropriate context. That means each sentence must be considered within the larger literary unit or *pericope* of which it is a part; each pericope must be read against the whole chapter in which it occurs; and chapters have meaning within the book in which they are found. Ultimately, as Jesus says to Satan, the context of each statement in scripture is the *whole of scripture*. When we speak of the Bible as the word of God, we are saying it is the whole book, all together, that is God's word to us—not any isolated verse or phrase, chapter, or book within it. We may pull out a favorite verse or chapter and use it for guidance, but unless we study deeply and broadly the *whole* of scripture, we run the danger of misinterpreting that passage by not seeing how it fits within the whole counsel of God. Without reading a whole passage, chapter, book, and the Bible, we may miss essential emphases that will confront and challenge us when we follow the narrow path of our favorite picks! So, when we read our Bibles, it is not as simple as opening it randomly and letting our finger fall on the passage of the day or moment. We need to know how the passage our finger selects fits within the whole word of God that is our Bible. We do that by reading every passage in its context.

THE UNITY FACTOR

The next factor is closely related to the previous one. Since scripture as a whole is the word of God, we can assume the essential *unity* of its intended message. We may talk about the theology of John or Paul or the author of the Letter to the Hebrews, and this is certainly part of reading the verses and passages of these bodies of literature in their appropriate context. However, I remain convinced that together all the individual pieces of scripture provide us with a unified understanding of the nature and purposes of God; we *can* construct a theology of the whole Bible. This does not mean, however, that there are *no conflicts or tensions* within the text of scripture. What the *unity factor* suggests is that, because the same God stands behind all scripture, what he is doing in each part has a certain overall unity when considered as a whole. What God was accomplishing through Israel and her sacrificial system in the Old Testament is the same thing he is accomplishing through the church and Christ's sacrificial death according to the New Testament. As a result, our understanding of God's word in scripture must be developed from an intimate knowledge of the *whole* of scripture: Old and New Testaments; Gospels, Letters, and Revelation; History, Wisdom, and Song of Songs. Individual passages achieve their purpose within the context of the whole, and understanding of key themes and concepts will involve us in the exploration of the breadth of scriptural teaching on the matter.

This certainly makes our approach to scripture more difficult than simply reading the verse or passage of the day seeking for God's directive. We may get directives in this manner, and I am not knocking devotional reading of the Bible! But our narrow reading can be misleading unless it is paralleled by consistent attention to the depth and breadth of the Bible to provide context for our devotional moments. This sort of depth reading can take a lifetime! And that is the challenge—to dedicate ourselves to the lifelong process of becoming more and more competent interpreters of scripture.

THE PARAMETER FACTOR

Although scripture is a unified literary construct that must be read as a whole in order to hear the whole counsel of God, any reading that allows scripture to speak for itself will have to face the fact that many tensions stand unresolved within scripture. Which Gospel order of events is accurate? Matthew? Mark? Luke? How do we hold Proverbs' assumption that God gives blessing and prosperity to the righteous together with Job's clear testimony that the righteous often suffer inexplicably? Does God *not change his mind* (Numbers 23:19; 1 Samuel 15:29), or *does* he (Exodus 32:12–14)? Any close reading of scripture as a unity is going to have to deal with these tensions and many, many more!

When faced by oppositions such as these, often our natural tendency is to resolve the tension either by explaining it away or by rejecting one of the offending opposites. This, however, makes *us the master of scripture* rather than allowing it to master us. I would much rather have a word of God that is my authority than assert my own authority over the word of God! I know how flawed and mistaken my own perceptions and understandings can sometimes be. One of the first ways forward in the face of scriptural tensions is to realize that all tension is not bad. In fact, much tension is absolutely necessary. I like to think of it like a balloon filled with air or helium. It is, in fact, the tension of gas pressing out in all directions that give the balloon its shape. Without these tensions, the balloon would have no shape at all. Similarly, scripture is full of tensions that give it shape and meaning. Without these tensions, the shape of scripture—and our theology—would be radically different from what God intends it to be.

With all its tensions, scripture is the territory where our faith is to be formed, challenged, shaped, and expanded. God is both just and merciful. God saves and yet destroys. The righteous prosper, and they perish. And scripture stands as witness that true faith must be lived out within the parameters represented by these truths. Sure, if tensions press far enough, a balloon eventually pops! But the balloon of scripture has not exploded yet, regardless of all its tensions. Those who under the influence of the Holy Spirit selected and affirmed the many traditions of scripture provided us with the biblical balloon with its particular shape and oppositions. Our job is to accept that shape and live in the light of it. Its tensions may challenge our assumptions and stretch our limits, but we will be better disciples for living in tension rather than opting for the easier way of harmonizing away or chopping off what does not fit into *our* understanding.

THE INCARNATIONAL FACTOR

There is a certain parallel between Jesus as the incarnate word of God and the nature of scripture. In both, the divine revelation of God is made manifest in human form. Jesus was both human and God bound together. In his humanness, Jesus took on certain limitations of his divine character (Philippians 2:5–8). His divine glory was cloaked so that he did not destroy humans upon contact (cf. Exodus 33:11–23). During his earthly life, Jesus had to breathe, eat, drink, and eliminate just like all other humans. He spoke Hebrew, walked from place to place, got tired, and lived out his life within the narrow confines of first century A.D. Jewish culture. Because of the limitations of his humanity, Jesus could be (and often was!) misunderstood. The common people thought he was a great prophet—perhaps the messiah. His enemies thought he was a blasphemer in league with Satan. Even his closest disciples were not completely certain who he was. And his family thought at times he was crazy!

The parallel with scripture is clear. God chose to reveal his enduring testimony to his work in the world in human words—Hebrew, Aramaic, and Greek. These words, as we have seen, share all the limitations and ambiguities of all other human words. They can be misunderstood, misinterpreted, distorted, and rejected. The God-ness of the Bible is not so apparent that everyone who reads it is forced to acknowledge its claims.

We also need to remember that it is *Jesus* who is the word of God. He is the fullest revelation of God's nature and purpose ever made manifest in terms humans could see and understand. Scripture, on the other hand, is not *the* word of God on the same order as Jesus, but becomes God's word as it testifies to the purpose of God in the world as fulfilled in the life and words of the incarnate man. Scripture is not even a complete account of all the events of Jesus' life. Those few events selected have been chosen to point us toward faith in the true incarnate Word of God (John 20:30–31). Our Bibles must be interpreted, because they are very human documents enabled by the guiding power of the Holy Spirit to point beyond themselves to the living and incarnate word of God, Jesus. The scriptures are theological documents that, when read in the light of the Holy Spirit, can convict us of sin and lead us into a saving relationship with God through Jesus.

THE CANONICAL FACTOR

The final factor arises from the fact that our Bibles are more than documents that fell from heaven completely formed from the pen of God. They are, instead, documents that have been selected, preserved, authorized, and treasured by the believing community of faith. There is not enough space to talk extensively about the process by which the traditions of the community of faith became written documents, books, and finally an authoritative canon—an exclusive list of authoritative books to serve as the foundation and guide of our faith. But it is clear that the believing community of faith stood at the heart of this extended process.

The canonical process involved selection and rejection. We know of many ancient and revered documents that were not included in the authorized canon. Those that *were* chosen were included, because in them the canonizers heard the word of God spoken in ways that were consistent with the teaching of the ancestral bearers of tradition, the eyewitnesses, and the apostles.

The creation of the canon has implications for how we interpret canonical scripture. First, the creation of canon gives this group of books an exclusive authority. Enoch and Jubilees may be books of great interest and even spiritual insight, but they are not canon. Second, it is the *canonical form* of the biblical books that is the authority for life, not any reconstruction of an earlier layer or more original document. Despite all the insight and understanding brought to the study of scripture by the methods of historical criticism, it is finally the text of scripture as affirmed by the canonizers that provides the parameters of the balloon within which our faith is to be lived out. Only as we allow the canonical shape of scripture to challenge our assumptions and presumptions rather than shaping the canon to *our* understanding of its truth do we allow the Bible to act as the authoritative word of God to us. Otherwise we get to set the agenda and determine the playing field.

This is certainly not to say the issue of canon and authority is an easy one. For one thing, the canon has always had "fuzzy" edges. The ancient rabbis who discussed the closure of the Hebrew canon at the end of the first century A.D. had differences of opinion about the inclusion of books like Ecclesiastes and Esther. The Greek translation of the Hebrew Bible included fourteen or so additional books (the Apocrypha) that did not make the cut into the authoritative Hebrew version. Catholics traditionally recognize those books as part of scripture, while Protestants exclude them. If we look to the canons of the Eastern Orthodox Church or the Egyptian Coptic Church, we find other differences as well.

And the debates don't end there. We continue to debate the authority and value of one book or another. The German Protestant theologian Martin Luther was none too happy that the book of James was in the canon, since it seemed to teach salvation through works rather than by faith alone. Luther could not remove James from the canon, but he did relegate it to an unnumbered appendix in his German translation of the Bible. We too often form similar "canons within the canon" when we simply ignore reading certain books or passages because they do not fit well with our Christian understanding.

These fuzzy edges of the canon are an indication of the human nature of the Bible and of the whole process of canonization. It is only through the power of the Holy Spirit that God can ensure that his will and purpose is carried out and his guidance is available to those who read with eyes of faith. We should also be encouraged to read and interpret in an attitude of humility. If God ensures that his saving message is communicated despite this diversity of canonical formulations, then we ought to allow ourselves to be challenged through dialogue with those who hold another form of the canon. Our purpose ought to be to know God and not to defend our own particular view of the canon. Thus Protestants ought to be able to dialogue with Catholics about what dimensions the Apocryphal books bring to the life of faith.

CONCLUSION OF THE MATTER

Now that we have completed our tour of factors behind the interpretation of the Bible, you should have a better idea of how to answer the question with which this chapter began: "Why do we interpret the Bible?" While the Bible is the word of God, it is revealed in very human words and language. The meaning of the Bible is shaped by the original Hebrew, Aramaic, and Greek languages in which it is written and by the cultures that spoke those languages and transmitted their traditions in written form.

There is one more issue, however, that I would like to make clear. Too often my students assume that interpretation of scripture is simply a matter of opinion. In an age of extreme tolerance, we tend to assume that every opinion or interpretation is equally valid. Biblical interpretation as described in this chapter is committed to discovering the "better" or "most appropriate" interpretation of a passage and of scripture as a whole. Scripture is more than just a springboard from which we take off into some sort of free-form reverie of personal reflection or emotional experience. If scripture is to challenge our assumptions and presumptions—if scripture is to be the authority of our lives—then we must accept that it has a message it intends to impart to the reader and that there are better and worse interpretations of that message. The tools discussed in this chapter are ways of ensuring scripture remains free from our manipulation to speak clearly to us in life-changing ways.

I also hope this discussion serves to answer the question that is at the heart of this book: What are they teaching at that college anyway? As you can see, our goal is to assist students in taking the Bible seriously as the source of authority for their lives. To do this they must become active interpreters of scripture and not just passive readers or, even worse, readers whose vision is narrowed by a set of presumptive blinders. Students can leave college with a set of tools for biblical interpretation, but it takes a lifetime of consistent practice to hone those skills into an effective and faithful practice of reading and listening to the will and purpose of God embedded there. It is our hope that our students will take on this challenge and live lives increasingly shaped by the word of God.

THE GUIDE TO LIFE?

Let me try to draw this discussion together with an illustrative example that indicates the need for biblical interpretation and suggests the complexity of the enterprise. All of us as Christians need guidance in our lives. We believe that scripture is the source of divine guidance for us. We often turn there for understanding how to live our lives day by day—at least we certainly ought to. One of the most popular books many Christians turn to for such guidance is the book of Proverbs. These brief statements have a breath of truth about them—they often accord with our own experience. There is a problem, however, with the way we most often employ them. Frequently we treat these proverbial sayings as if they are individual nuggets of gold—absolute truth. We tend to take them out of context and apply them indiscriminately to our lives and to others.

Take Proverbs 22:6, for example: "Train a child in the way he should go, and when he is old he will not turn from it." Is there an absolute cause and effect relationship between parenting and the development of humans? Is this a divine *promise* that parents can always rely on? How many good parents have been broken on the rock of this proverb wrongly applied? How many have agonized over where they went wrong in raising a particularly rebellious child or a fallen adult son or daughter? This sort of response is to misunderstand the nature of proverbial truth—observational truth. Observation tells us that parents who fail to train their children in what is right and wrong often experience the pain of a wayward child. The proverb is a true observation of *some circumstances in life*. However, you cannot reverse a proverb by saying that if a child goes wrong, his parents *must* have failed in their parenting. Children are free agents and can make wrong decisions regardless of their upbringing. Sometimes there are other influences on children that parenting, no matter how good, just cannot overcome.

The fallacy of reading proverbs as individual nuggets of universal truth is revealed by a careful reading of scripture as a whole. According to Proverbs 12:21, for example, the righteous can anticipate a carefree life: "No harm befalls the righteous, but the wicked have their fill of trouble." But careful attention to the whole of scripture (and personal experience) makes it clear that righteousness is no sure protection against trouble and suffering. Job is righteous, but he suffered horrendously. His friends could not accept his righteousness because his suffering seemed to contradict it. Their theology was grounded in statements like Proverbs 12:21. But at the end of the book, it is the *friends* who are rebuked by God because "you have not spoken of me what is right, as my servant Job has" (Job 42:7).

Individual proverbs are not absolute truth by themselves. They are not even the word of God when read *alone*! It is the Bible read as a whole that is God's word to us, and individual proverbs find their appropriate place in God's truth to us when we read them alongside the rest of the book of Proverbs and scripture as a whole. Similarly, single verses or passages of scripture are the word of God only in concert with the whole of the Bible. That is why it is so important to gain a thorough knowledge of the great expanse of scripture—both Old and New Testaments—in order to understand what God is teaching us in any part of it.

5

OLD TESTAMENT: CONGREGATION AND ACADEMY SHARE A WHOLE BIBLE, NOT JUST A HALF

William Yarchin

If the congregation and academy are divided, surely one point of contention revolves around interpretation of scripture. In this chapter we will explore that apparent divide. Our primary focus will rest on the Old Testament; similar issues with particular reference to the New Testament will be taken up in the next chapter. We will find that the seeming differences between congregation and college classroom over biblical interpretation arise because the two exist for different (though related) purposes and so use the Bible in different (though related) ways. We will illuminate those "related differences" by pointing out the answers to very basic questions about the Bible one usually receives from the church on the one hand and the university on the other. Ultimately we will find that respect for these differences can actually result in mutual edification, enhancing the Bible as God's word for both pulpit and podium in today's society. Between the two, it is a whole Bible that is read, not just a half.

FIRST VERY BASIC QUESTION: WHAT IS THE BIBLE?

Christians of the evangelical persuasion typically live out their lives without wandering very far from the Bible. They hear it preached from, they quote it, they meditate upon it—they even commit small portions of it to memory. And when they go off to college, most of these evangelical Christians find themselves enrolled in required Bible classes. From such students you would expect a well-informed answer when asked, "What is the Bible?"

More often than not, however, the answer is rather lopsided. Most Christian students have not been confronted with this question put forth quite so boldly. Usually their relationship with scripture is rather non-analytic, so a question like this rarely arises in a serious vein. Consequently many of them do not know how to respond to the question. Others, who are not as intimidated by the question, are quick to endorse the Bible's spiritual attributes: "inspired word of God," "an infallible guide to salvation," "God's love letters to us," "the source of absolute truth," and so on. Doctrinally and devotionally sound answers, to be sure. But note that such expressions are not statements of fact with which everyone universally would immediately agree. Rather they are faith claims to which only fellow believers would assent. In other words, when faced with the question of what the Bible is, Christians' default answers are usually lopsided toward faith claims and somewhat lacking in factual statements.

Of course, within the boundaries of the believing community, "the Bible is the word of God" does not usually stir up controversy. Beyond the confines of our faith groups, though, that claim, and all others like it, can be challenged. For many people the Bible is not the inspired word of God or the source of absolute truth. The inspiration and truth of scripture are not universally recognized facts. In answering our question about the Bible are we then restricted to faith claims intelligible only to fellow believers? If our faith claims are not accepted, is the entire worth of the Bible thereby negated? Are there no factual statements about the Bible that can be made beyond the horizon of faith?

To this last question the answer is yes, certainly. There is plenty of value that can be found in the Bible apart from faith claims. The Bible's linguistic, literary, and historical dimensions—that is, the nuances of its original ancient languages, the history of its composition, the range and complexity of materials that make it up—are universally observable. Here's an unwieldy chain of several such factual statements: The Bible is a collection / of many different writings / produced in (at least) three different languages / by many different writers / using many different literary styles / during many different historical eras / addressing many different circumstances. These facets of the Bible can be studied universally, within the community of faith and beyond its boundaries as well. From such study a lot of uncontroversial, factual statements can be made about the Bible that require no faith for assent. One need not be a Christian to affirm such claims.

The lopsidedness of our "faith-only" approach to the Bible is a reflection of a certain "ghetto-ization" of our evangelical Christian discourse. My use of the term *ghetto* is not necessarily negative. It refers to an insular community of inhabitants that largely have to do with themselves in certain key relationships, engaging minimally with the outside world. Ghetto life is often marked by the development of a dialect that is spoken among the residents of a ghetto and not well understood by those living outside. It is this specific sense of the word that I intend. Among ourselves in our evangelical circles, we know what we mean when we use in-house phrases like "inspired word of God" or just "God's word." In "evangelicaleze" language, reference to the Bible rarely has to do with its plainly factual dimension. At church we read the Old Testament largely for a direct spiritual application of truth to our lives, something that is available only to faith and is expressible only in faith language. If we were to read the Bible as believers who participate in a broader range of civic and cultural discourse in society—beyond the walls of our ghetto—we would be fluent in both dialects, faith and fact. A full-bodied answer to our question "What is the Bible?" would not lean so one-sidedly to the faith dimension of scripture.

IT'S MORE THAN THAT

When we study the Bible, then, are we studying the whole Bible? I am not asking whether we include both the Old and New Testaments in our Bible. I am asking whether our embrace of the Bible is restricted to its faith dimension alone or whether we also factor in the demonstrably factual elements of what the Bible is when we read it. The answer to that question is linked closely to the various settings in which we use scripture.

A college classroom is not the same setting as a church worship service or a youth group Bible study. This is why, compared with what they are accustomed to, Christian students often find themselves faced with a different set of vocabulary, questions, and even presuppositions when the Bible is discussed in Christian university classes. It may be the same church Bible opened on the classroom desk, but the student is closely studying a map of ancient Jerusalem as well as the psalmist's thanksgiving for the city's protection. The Old Testament professor strives to build faith, but instead of hearing a sermon the students get challenging lectures about linguistic nuances underlying the laws of Moses. Students are introduced to new ways of thinking and talking about the Bible—ways that are more universally intelligible, in both the sacred and secular spheres of modern life. They learn that the Bible has inherent value on the basis of facts as well as of faith. Just as they themselves do not exist exclusively in a single faith-dimension, they learn that the Bible doesn't either. The college classroom is where students learn more fully dimensioned answers to the question, "What is the Bible?"

This makes sense. People do not go to college simply to be edified. We seek to become better equipped with skills for life. That is why students declare areas of major study, so that they can enter society as adults who contribute and participate in society with their thinking and their working. So also with the Bible. As graduates that enter into society with professional and confessional orientation, Christians are better equipped to understand the Bible and to bring its vision into their society if they have become acquainted with its elements that speak from a faith informed by fact.

SECOND VERY BASIC QUESTION: WHAT IS IN THE BIBLE?

Here again, what you might expect from dedicated evangelical Christian college students (on the one hand) and what you discover in conversation with them (on the other) are not always the same thing. In my experience, students of this sort sincerely believe the faith claims we have been discussing. They hold the Bible in high regard for its authority and inspiration. Often they may be very familiar with select small portions of it. But for all their devotion to the Bible, evangelical Christian students arriving at college tend to be oddly ignorant of its actual contents.

They are often quite aware, for example, of the importance of Genesis for any Christian understanding of the world's origins. Yet few are the students who have ever actually read *all* Old Testament creation passages methodically, in context. Christian students have staked their souls on the efficacy of Christ's death and the power of his resurrection. Yet they know of these events and their significance not from a first-hand encounter with New Testament documents, but largely from what they have been told by their Christian teachers.

There is nothing necessarily wrong with this state of affairs. For centuries great masses of dedicated Christians have followed their Lord without having read or studied the scriptures for themselves. This has been true particularly in times and places where literacy has not been very widespread. The good news proclaims that salvation does not depend on education or even on literacy.

But when the task is a university education at a Christian institution, it will not do to simply learn things *about* the Bible. A superior liberal arts education is one in which students engage directly with the primary sources. This applies to studies in philosophy, where students learn for themselves what Plato said, and in English, where there is no substitute for reading Shakespeare for oneself. So also with the Bible. Actually, even more so, given the key role scripture plays in our knowledge of God—particularly for us in the Protestant wing of the church. Interestingly, once our evangelical students become aware of the rich textures found in scripture they often become ideal, highly motivated students, precisely because of (and not in spite of) their devotional attachment to the Bible.

For this reason a good general studies program at many Christian institutions can include as many as three courses in biblical studies. Students read the Old Testament foundation story of salvation, and likewise in the New Testament, and cap off their Bible requirement with a course chosen from a rather wide-ranging menu of Bible courses. By designing a Bible curriculum to cover the fullest possible range of scripture, Christian faculties seek to avoid imposing one portion of the Bible over others. Thus we attempt to read Old Testament texts without the expectation that they must always sound like New Testament texts. Otherwise we risk missing the rich texture of the full scriptural witness to God's truth. Our Bible courses operate from the assumption that, for sound education in a Christian setting, nothing substitutes for a direct engagement with the biblical texts themselves.

The study of scripture within this framework is inductive in method, which means that the features of the texts themselves (rather than the demands of contemporary cultural trends) are taken as the primary indication for how the texts are to be interpreted. So, for example, if in a given passage the Bible presents us with a poem—as is frequently the case in the Old Testament—we acknowledge that fact (there's that word!) and tune our interpretive ear to the ways poetry communicates. Similarly, we would seek to understand the words of scripture in keeping with the ancient cultural and linguistic context in which they were written. *Inductive method*: following the text to its meaning according to its own signals instead of automatically reading into it the meaning we have already determined for it according to our perspective. We could also call it Old Testament criticism, which is simply another way of saying biblical discernment: studying the biblical text with a discerning eye for genre, historical context, language, and so forth.

WHY IT'S HARD TO SEE WITH YOUR GLASSES ON

Most evangelical Christians would agree with the approach to the study of scripture outlined here, at least in principle. For all its appeal, however, inductive text-driven study of the Bible poses at least two serious challenges to eager Christian students who resolve to read the Bible—particularly the Old Testament—for what it has to say on its own terms.

First of all, it is not easy to do. None of us comes to the Bible utterly devoid of any assumptions as to what we are going to find. As Christian scripture the text of the Bible does not lie before us completely free of any influence exerted by our own Christian and denominational perspectives. All of us pick up the Bible wearing a set of glasses, as it were, through which the Bible is read in the way that seems most fitting or natural to us. Those glasses are a metaphor I am using to designate the presuppositions, biases, and inherited interpretive traditions that affect the way we understand the text. For some of us they are Baptist glasses. For others they are Methodist, or American, or male, or female, or middle-class, or modern glasses. They are assumptions we make about what the text must mean given the upbringing we have experienced and, very often, the things we have been told the Bible must say. When we approach it with those glasses on, the Old Testament sounds familiar, saying to us the things we have come to expect it from it.

There is nothing inherently wrong with reading the Old Testament through a set of "traditioned" assumptions or biases. In fact, we cannot help but read from some perspective. I cannot easily read the Bible from a female point of view, for example, inasmuch as I happen to be male (I tend to wear male glasses when I read the Old Testament). But if we are going to attempt to hear the Bible speak on its own terms, we can at least recognize that we do wear our glasses and take that into account when we study the Bible. We can, to some extent, take them off and hear the text afresh. The methods of inductive Bible study are designed to help accomplish precisely that: to help remove the glasses as much as possible. Far from posing a threat to the Bible's status as scripture, such methods directly support our evangelical claims about the Bible as the authoritative word of God. For if the Bible is the authority and not we ourselves, we are well advised to dial into the Bible's own signals as to how it is to be read. Otherwise our commitment can be off target, focusing on what our glasses show us rather than on what scripture tells us. Inductive method in Bible study definitely helps keep us on course.

Sounds great. How hard could this be? Well, most of us have never experienced the Bible apart from some context that predisposes a rather pedantic set of interpretations. In Sunday church services, Wednesday evening Bible studies, youth groups, devotional small groups—our usual encounters with scripture are typically focused toward a targeted outcome.

This has the effect of "setting up" certain interpretations as automatically "normal" or "correct" while all others are dismissed. The possibility is not considered that a biblical passage might, on its own terms apart from the immediate agenda of application to our lives, point to a different meaning than our customary one. By virtue of their familiarity, interpretations of the Bible that our glasses help produce seem natural to the text, as though we weren't wearing glasses at all. That is why it is often difficult to remove them, because usually we aren't aware that we are wearing them. Letting the text speak for itself, free from our expectations of what it surely must mean, calls for the discipline of following sound inductive method with an open mind. Easier said than done.

THE CHALLENGE OF DIRECT
OLD TESTAMENT ENGAGEMENT

Let me illustrate from a detail in an Old Testament passage. The stories of the Hebrew ancestors tell us that Abram and his wife Sarai were too old to have children, although God had promised that Abram would have descendants. In Genesis 16 we learn that Abram's household included a slave woman from Egypt named Hagar. According to ancient Semitic custom, a woman in Hagar's position would be part of the property that makes up Abram's household, over which he would have absolute authority. The Bible tells us that Sarai suggested that Abram sleep with Hagar as a sexual surrogate (as ancient custom permitted), with the expectation that children—heirs—would thereby be born to the household. Abram did so, and sure enough Hagar became pregnant: "And he had sex with Hagar, and she conceived; and when she saw that she had conceived, she had less respect for her mistress" (Genesis 16:4). Hagar's attitude was too much for Sarai. With Abram's permission she began to treat Hagar so harshly that the slave woman fled in desperation into the desert, at great risk to her life and the life of her unborn child.

The story goes on from here, but I want to draw attention to the way we tend to understand verse four, with glasses on: If Hagar was pregnant, and Sarai remained barren, then Hagar's loss of respect for Sarai was obviously an expression of pride over her own privileged (pregnant) status. That is, Hagar became prideful and sought to exploit her new position as the carrier of Abram's seed at Sarai's expense. This understanding of Hagar's attitude toward Sarai is the default position. It is so common that it has even found its way into a recent English translation: "Later, when Hagar knew she was going to have a baby, she became proud and was hateful to Sarai" (Contemporary English Version).

But the tensions between Hagar and Sarai may be of a different sort. Hagar is a female foreigner who subsists in Abram's household without any power of her own, as the story clearly indicates. Let us take off our glasses and consider: When the master of the household impregnates a powerless, foreign, female worker through uninvited sex while the wife is fully aware but does nothing—in fact, the wife is complicit in the deed—wouldn't the wife lose respect in the slave's eyes? In such a scenario Hagar's disrespect would reflect her hurt over Sarai's betrayal rather than any arrogance over Sarai's barrenness.

Either reading of the episode is permitted by the text in its cultural context. But with our glasses on—our assumptions about Abram's virtue, our tradition of identifying with Abram and Sarai as heroes of the story, our custom of *not* reading from a female slave's point of view—the more "natural" reading seems *so* natural we may even translate "pride and arrogance" into the text where the Bible itself says no such thing. While the text permits either reading, our glasses (and sometimes our modern translations) have already decided which one we'll adopt. That's not letting the Bible speak for itself. That's having our traditions and our prejudices speak for the Bible. In this case, our prejudiced reading of a "haughty Hagar" could bring us to impugn the character of women in our own world who have been sexually victimized. Uncritical (undiscerning) study of the Old Testament can have very unchristian consequences. If as Christians we are called to hear and understand the word of God, surely our vocation includes the obligation to carefully consider textually warranted interpretations, even when—especially when!—our familiar cultural assumptions might be challenged. The word of God tends to do just that: call us and move us toward changing evermore into the image of Christ.

Okay, so we do our best and remove our glasses somewhat when we study the Old Testament. Then the second major challenge confronts us. We begin to encounter elements, very strange elements, in the Old Testament that we didn't notice as much when we were wearing our glasses. Consider, for example, the Hagar passage we just mentioned. In our world, we don't have slaves, and we don't have sex with them in order to ensure that we have heirs. But the Bible presents these details of the episode without comment on the strangeness of it all. Virtually every page of the Old Testament presents these sorts of challenges.

This is because of another fact: The books of the Old Testament were not written for our world or to our world or in our world. The writers produced these books in languages and in cultural and historical horizons quite different from ours. Because they were not writing to us in our world, they did not feel it was necessary to add footnotes or maps or other aids for interpretation. Indeed, the very presence of these tools in our present-day study Bibles and commentaries demonstrates the inherent foreignness of the Old Testament. When we turn to these tools we are actually attempting to take our glasses off and enter into the world of the biblical writers to the extent that we can.

Beyond the strangeness of ancient customs, perhaps a far greater challenge confronts us as we remove our glasses and realize what the Old Testament has to say about God. While most Bible readers will take certain poetic theological expressions in stride ("smoke went up from his nostrils, and devouring fire from his mouth," Psalm 18:8), in other Old Testament passages the Bible does not always match our theological preconceptions. Unfamiliar geography and ancient laws and even poetic expression—these we can handle. But when it comes to ways of understanding God (isn't that why we read the Bible in the first place?), the Old Testament can floor us.

Let us take, for example, the golden calf episode as narrated in Exodus 32. While Moses was atop Mount Sinai receiving the law from God, the people of Israel had decided to worship a golden calf as their deity. Their action, of course, flagrantly violated their own agreement with God to exclusive worship, their commitment to forsake idols. God's reaction to this betrayal was extreme, as he angrily told Moses that he (God) would destroy all the people of Israel. Only Moses would be spared. Moses then engaged God in a reconsideration of this death penalty, with an outcome that never fails to surprise students when they read the text for themselves: Upon hearing what Moses had to say, "the Lord changed his mind about the disaster that he had planned to bring on his people" (32:14, NRSV). Students are taken aback by what the text here plainly says. They are struck by the difference between what they have thought the Bible says about God and what they can read for themselves, with glasses removed.

First of all, we tend to assume that the biblical God already knows everything in advance. But here it seems that he doesn't. If God already knew that he would not actually destroy the people of Israel, then he clearly wasn't angry enough to wipe them out, even though this is what the text says. Second, there is this detail about God changing his mind. Again, if God already knows everything in advance, then how can God change his mind about anything? Isn't God's will immutable, unchanging?

As it turns out, the Old Testament rather consistently shows us a deity who indeed does change his mind about actions he had previously decided to carry out. The general pattern is this: When there is change on earth, such as repentance, there is (the possibility of) change in heaven, with God's turning away from intended judgment. This pattern is so characteristic of the biblical God that it constitutes the whole premise for the plot of the book of Jonah: God does not move toward judgment in a blind rage but remains open to factors that warrant grace instead of judgment. Indeed, it is this pattern that underlies the good news of Christ's redemption according to Christian doctrine. Change on earth (a person's repentance and faith in Christ) actualizes for that person a divine change: a turning from judgment to adoption of the repentant sinner as a child of God. Notwithstanding our shock at reading the golden calf episode, the changing of God's mind in that story from judgment to mercy is wholly in keeping with the nature of the God we worship as Christians!

It's just that the Old Testament offers insights into God's nature in ways not immediately intelligible to us. The ancient writers did not produce theological treatises featuring a systematic use of clearly defined terms. As a result the Old Testament is no theological textbook. Rather, it exists as a collection of stories, songs, laws, prophetic utterances (in poetic form), genealogies, and so forth. Here again we are simply acknowledging a fact about the Bible—a fact that must be taken into account for a full-orbed answer to the question, "What is in the Bible?"

When we recognize this fact we can see another one relevant to our first very basic question: The Bible is not the same thing as the body of Christian doctrine. Christian teaching about God's nature, God's relationship to humans and to the world, and God's purpose for our lives is not found systematically spelled out in the Bible. In fact, some tensions do exist between texts and between Testaments in Christian scripture. Biblical interpretation from a Christian perspective often involves itself with making intertextual connections—links that the texts themselves will support—leading to a coherent body of theological teaching. Christian doctrine, then, has emerged from generations of careful reflection on what the biblical poems, stories, laws, etc. altogether present to us about God. The mistake that we often make—and that sets us up for a shock when we take off our glasses—is to assume that when we open up the Bible we are reading a book in which Christian doctrine is plainly and directly set forth. Not so, particularly when we open up the Old Testament. (See further in the hermeneutics chapter.)

THE OLD TESTAMENT, CHRISTIAN DOCTRINE, AND
DIFFERENT INSTITUTIONAL SETTINGS

What then is the relationship of the Bible to the systems of Christian doctrine that the church has constructed? First of all, we ought to realize that doctrine derives from scripture and not the other way around. It is scripture, not doctrine, that we accept as divinely inspired. Therefore it is scripture, not doctrine, that we accept as bearing divine authority. Unlike God's word, systems of Christian teaching flex and adjust through the centuries in keeping with the changing horizons of human knowledge and cultural reference points. During ancient times, doctrine was formulated in terms that made sense within the intellectual and cultural framework that prevailed at the time. During the modern era, Christian teaching has had to be reformulated in order to remain understandable. This revisionary process is a given, and it will by necessity continue as a major part of our calling to bring the Gospel to the world until Christ returns.

Following from this, we note that, second of all, changes in our doctrine are sometimes required in order to make our notions of God more faithfully aligned with the biblical testimony. This is where taking our glasses off enters the picture. Remember, with this metaphor we mean fresh study of scripture to hear it on its own terms, speaking to its own world, apart from what our traditions of Christian teaching and our cultural biases might require the Old Testament to say about God and humans. When we do this we can open our Bible reading to God's illumination of areas in our Christian teaching that aren't quite in tune with his word. In that sense, methodical glasses-free Bible study is no mere intellectual exercise. It becomes a critical part of spiritual discipline practiced in the body of Christ. A methodically informed approach to scripture supports our calling to follow Jesus as he teaches us—through our study of a whole, contextualized Bible—where we are obedient and where we are not yet obedient. Our calling is not simply to determine the meaning of scripture but ultimately to have it determine our meaning.

By way of illustration, suppose that Christians in the affluent West came to believe that our material abundance was the result of a divine-human agreement whereby being faithful to God automatically brings prosperity. With glasses firmly in place, we might read very selectively from the Old Testament, convinced that our quid pro quo theology is biblically sound: If we are good to God in the form of obedient piety, then God is obligated to be good to us in the form of material prosperity. Our experience of abundance, and the Old Testament verses that we quote, would confirm this belief, and it could become a part of what we teach in our churches. "The wicked earn no real gain, but those who sow righteousness get a true reward" (Proverbs 11:18). A glasses-off reading of *all* the Old Testament, however, would help correct this misguided doctrine. In the book of Job and many of the prophets, for example, we would find the Old Testament insisting that the biblical God cannot be domesticated into a convenient prop for prosperity. To be sure, the book of Job raises its own set of theological questions. But one claim that it decisively rejects is that human piety secures a divine guarantee of material wealth and perfect health.

In this example our doctrine will have been corrected toward a more biblically faithful expression of the nature of the God-human nexus. As Protestants we affirm that it is the Bible, and not our doctrinal system, that is the authoritative word of God. Therefore, glasses-free study of the Bible is not something we can do without. It is rather a practice the church must cultivate for the sake of the faithfulness and purity of its doctrine. But where? What is the proper setting for the sort of "whole Bible" study we have been talking about in this chapter?

There is probably no single correct answer to this question. Not everything that is proper for a church setting is suitable in the college setting and vice versa. A Christian college is a setting in which Christians learn how to participate professionally and culturally in the world beyond their church walls. This role for Christian university education is rarely taken to be in competition or at odds with the function of the church that supports the university. This same distinction in settings and roles applies as well to the study of the Bible: The way it is done in the Christian college classroom need not be in conflict with the use of the Bible in church. To the contrary, the church's modern mission in the world has benefited from the rigorous research in sociology, psychology, and global studies that is carried out at the university. So also with the Bible, the full-dimensioned study of scripture proper to a Christian university can provide to the church the sort of empowering intellectual foundation for contemporary application of the Bible not readily generated in any other setting.

Let me conclude with an example of this last point. In 1977 a Christian professor wrote a widely read book that has prompted the Christian church in the Western world to grapple with the moral evil of poverty. *Rich Christians in an Age of Hunger* grew out of author Ron Sider's academic study of the Bible. In his book Sider drew attention to the biblical laws directing God's people to tithe directly to the economically marginalized people among them, asking what that might mean for contemporary Christians who enjoy abundant financial harvests. Surveying biblical passages from the Old and New Testaments, Sider also pointed out a consistent theological pattern: God will not only bring judgment upon the rich who exploit and oppress the poor, but also stands against the prosperous when they simply fail to help the poor. Sider's book forcefully noted that the biblical God has a huge concern for the economically disadvantaged and that God's people have a moral duty to share that concern and to find ways of helping the poor. The distinctive challenge of *Rich Christians* lies in Sider's claim that, if Christians are to be obediently responsive to the biblical portrayal of God's heart for the poor, we must go beyond charitable giving. We must work to change the financial and social systems that perpetuate poverty throughout the world.

The publication of *Rich Christians* triggered an explosion of interest in the relationship of Christian faith and economic policy on the part of Christian economists. Many of Sider's specific economic proposals have been questioned, but through the book's four editions what has remained least revised, most enduring, and perhaps most challenging is the book's examination of biblical texts. One prominent economist, Carl M. Gambs, now a senior vice president at the Federal Reserve Bank, attributes the deliberately Christian attitude he has maintained in his career performance as an economist—his calling—in part to the influence of Sider's book while he was a student. For more than twenty-five years Christian students and their churches have been similarly urged in Sider's classrooms and by his books to examine their economics and lifestyles under the Bible's spotlight on the poor. Sider's "whole Bible" reading of scriptural teaching about wealth and poverty has been a prompt from the academy to the church toward a more complete Christian engagement with the world. Reciprocally, the church's mission in the world has provided direction and purpose for the scholar's faithfully factual study of scripture. The congregation and academy can both respond more effectively to Jesus' discipleship call when they share a whole Bible.

6

THE ACADEMIC SIDE OF
NEW TESTAMENT STUDIES

Keith H. Reeves and Kenneth L. Waters Sr.

THE BIBLE IN CULTURE AND THE CLASSROOM

Many students come to undergraduate biblical studies with some background in scripture as a result of upbringing in committed Christian families or strong personal faith commitments. Others come without much background in the Bible. However, even in this case their beliefs may well be strongly influenced by the Bible simply through participation in Western culture. In virtually all cases, Bible study in the university proves to be quite different from what students are accustomed to in the church or from what they have been exposed to in the public arena. Regardless of their level of exposure to scripture, then, students may share a common disorienting experience in the biblical studies classroom.

Most people who approach scripture from a faith commitment are accustomed to what may be called a devotional approach to the Bible. They have learned to read the Bible for "what God has to say to me or us." In this case, the Bible is the word of God read for spiritual and moral guidance, personal or corporate salvation, emotional support and healing, and improvement in life at one level or another. They have also learned to read the Bible for divinely revealed information about the past, present, and future. This way of reading the Bible is certainly one we affirm. In fact, our suggestions below are aimed at, among other things, enriching a devotional reading of scripture.

DIFFERENT READINGS

It should be noted that a devotional approach to the Bible is one that assumes a prior commitment to scripture's validity. However, how do we speak about the Bible when we move beyond the church walls and en-counter people who do not read the Bible devotionally, if they read it at all? Despite the Bible's influence in modern society, there are many who do not share the belief that the Bible is the word of God. For some the Bible may be great literature or a notable relic of the past, but no more than that. For others the Bible may be of no interest at all. We interact with these people on a daily basis, and, at times, we are challenged by these people and their ways of reading (or not reading) the Bible. Even among those of us who in-vest the Bible with some degree of authority, there is still disagreement over what the Bible is and what it means. In either case, the question then be-comes, "How do we respond to those who bring a different or opposing view of the Bible?"

It would be very easy to simply affirm what we have been taught and what we have come to believe in regard to the Bible. However, this simply reinforces the common (and wrong-headed) notion that different views of scripture are only opinions and that we have no objective handles for dis-cussing or resolving differences. Moreover, when we simply repeat what we already believe about scripture, we are only preaching to the choir (if speak-ing to those who already agree with us) or simply closing off discussion (if speaking to those who disagree with us). Neither option is very helpful for those of us who are learning to be world citizens, bridge-builders, peace-makers, and social healers. We must find a way to speak to others about the Bible on a basis more comprehensive than what we have come to believe. In addition, it is never a bad idea to put our own beliefs up for examina-tion. This does not mean that we have to abandon our views. It only means that we must learn how to reflect on our current ideas about scripture, meet people where they are in their own views, and talk to them on the basis of some common ground. This in fact seems to be what Paul the apostle meant when he said, "I have become all things to all people, that I might by all means save some" (1 Corinthians 9:22 NRSV).

THE HISTORICAL AND LITERARY APPROACH

One major disorienting element of biblical studies in a university setting is the use of historical and literary approaches to the Bible. While historical and literary perspectives on scripture may not appear often in our familiar church settings, consideration of these elements is not out of line with the broader goals of Christianity. Indeed, asking literary and historical questions about scripture is intended to enable us to reflect on our understanding of scripture, speak to other believers who may have different interpretations, and enter into useful conversation with skeptics at the same time. These approaches are particularly helpful in this endeavor because they allow us to discover some things about the Bible we may not find in a purely devotional approach.

For many Christians, any approach that looks at scripture from a literary or historical vantage point might seem illegitimate because it seems to imply that the Bible, a book we often refer to as the Holy Bible, is *only* a historical-literary document. However, we would argue that we don't have to choose between the divine inspiration of scripture and its historical and literary nature. A quick glance through scripture will tell us why this is the case. At the beginning of scripture, the Hebrew people are a nomadic bunch with a religious system built around clans. Some centuries later, they become part of a Jewish kingdom with a centralized religious structure, and eventually they become a small religious and ethnic group within the Greek, and later Roman, empires. We even find historical movement in the New Testament itself. The Gospels record the life and words of Jesus, while the Acts and Epistles give us a picture of the church after Jesus' death, and we end with a picture of the persecuted church at the end of the first century in Revelation. We will speak more specifically about different literary types in the New Testament later in this chapter, but it is also clear from a quick glance through scripture that it contains a number of different types of writing. The point is that the Bible reflects the various settings in which God's people find themselves over hundreds of years, and it expresses its message through a very diverse range of literary forms. Thus, a historical-literary approach to scripture is not something we impose on scripture. Instead, it is something that the Bible, by its diversity of historical settings and literary forms, seems to require if we are to interpret it thoughtfully. A careful and thoughtful understanding of scripture and application of its teaching to our lives is, we believe, the aim of our devotional reading of scripture. When used correctly, then, the intent of a historical-literary method is not to replace a devotional approach to scripture but to inform and enhance it.

A HISTORICAL APPROACH TO THE NEW TESTAMENT

The writings of the New Testament can be categorized into four main types: Gospel, acts, Epistle, and apocalypse. Assuming that these categories are generally acceptable, how does the historical approach to the New Testament work? To help us get at this question by means of the Gospels, we would propose four important questions that we would ask of any saying, deed, or report that we encounter in a Gospel text. Those questions are:

1. What did it mean for Jesus and his audience?
2. What did it mean for the Gospel writer and his audience?
3. What did it mean for later generations of Christians?
4. What might it mean for me or us today?

The first three are the historical questions. The fourth is the question of contemporary relevance.

When dealing with the Gospels of Matthew, Mark, Luke, or John, we have probably heard sermons or mediations that have skipped the first three questions and jumped immediately to the fourth. Such presentations might be right on target about the meaning of a Gospel passage for today or they could also be horribly off target or maybe just shallow and superficial. So how do we know? If we admit that people can make the Bible mean almost anything that they want it to mean, are there any tests for distinguishing between good and bad interpretations? This is a main reason we should give adequate attention to the historical questions above. If we believe that the meaning Jesus intended for his audience is the benchmark we should use for interpreting his words and actions today, it seems obvious that these questions help establish parameters for what we should say about a Gospel text's meaning for us. They place some control on the conclusions that are drawn from a Gospel story and lay a responsible groundwork for how an interpreter answers the question of contemporary relevance. This does not mean that everyone will have the same answers to these questions, but it does mean that everyone will have the kind of answers that appear reasonable and defensible within the general perspective of a public discussion.

THE WORLD OF JESUS AND THE GOSPEL WRITERS

The first question—what did Jesus' words or action mean to Jesus and his audience?—takes us into the world of first-century Palestinian Jews living under the dominion of Rome. It is a world very different from our own, so we need to understand something about this world in order to understand what Jesus' words and deeds meant to his first audience. It is important to know what Jesus meant for them before we explore what he means for us. For example, does Jesus' statement "if anyone strikes you on the right cheek, turn the other also" (Matthew 5:39 NRSV) mean that we should become willing victims, or is it a survival tactic for an oppressed, outnumbered people whose hands are tied behind their back? Or does it mean something else altogether? The key to making a decision may be to understand what it would have meant for a Jewish freedom fighter to retaliate against an abusive Roman soldier. Retaliation may well have led to the destruction of the freedom fighter's family and village by the Roman army, something avoidable if only the freedom fighter had turned the other cheek.

The second question takes us into the world of the Gospel writers. This too was a world very different from our own. It was also a world different from the world of Jesus. At least thirty-five years have passed between the death of Jesus and the writing of the earliest Gospel. Furthermore, there is a cultural difference. The world of the Gospel writers appears to be more urban and cosmopolitan than that of Jesus. Furthermore, they are for the most part writing for a largely Gentile church composed of former pagans, an audience that did not exist during Jesus' lifetime. This is important, because these chronological and cultural differences affect how the Gospel writers applied the story of Jesus to their own times. Therefore, in the parable of the lost son (Luke 15:11–32), the youngest son may represent those wayward Jews of first-century Palestine who were attracted to Jesus, while the eldest son represents those Pharisees and scribes who resented their attraction to Jesus. However, for Luke, some decades later, a shift in meaning occurs. The youngest son represents those wayward gentiles attracted to the Pauline mission, while the eldest son represents the Jewish Jerusalem Christians who resented Paul's mission to the gentiles (Acts 15:1–29). My, how things can change. If it is this easy to slip into the role of the eldest son, maybe we need to examine ourselves a bit more carefully before criticizing unfamiliar ways of ministering to the "lost."

LATER GENERATIONS AND CONTEMPORARY TIMES

The third question—what did Jesus' words and actions mean to later generations of Christians?—brings us into dialogue with biblical interpreters who lived from the second to the fourth centuries. At this point, we leave the field of Gospel studies and enter the domain of church history. It is sometimes helpful to see how later generations of biblical interpreters who yet lived prior to our time explained biblical passages. Although this takes us beyond a direct engagement with the Bible, such a study shows the origins of some modern interpretations of the biblical text. For example, when Jesus told Peter, "on this rock I will build my church" (Matthew 16:18), who or what was he referring to? There is still a lot of debate surrounding this question. An obscure figure named Pseudo-Clement (second century) thought that the rock was Peter. Theodore of Mopsuestia (d. 428) said that the rock was Peter's confession. Augustine (d. 430) believed that the rock was Jesus himself. At least we can begin with a range of options when trying to make our own informed decision.

Since the book of Acts is a sequel to the Gospel of Luke and identical in style we ask the same historical questions about the book of Acts that we ask about Luke and the other Gospels; only this time the focus of the first question shifts from Jesus of Nazareth to the apostles of the Jewish and gentile Christian missions. What would a reported word, deed, or event have meant for the apostles and their original audiences? We must also still ask the next question about the meaning of these same reports for the author Luke, who may be writing about these matters as many as thirty-five years after they occurred and in some cases for an entirely different audience. Therefore, Paul's speech in Acts 17:22–31 to the philosophers of Athens on the unknown God was, in their perspective, a failed attempt at promoting a new philosophy, but for Luke and his audience at least fifteen years later, it was the emergence of Christianity as a new world religion.

In the New Testament Epistles and the book of Revelation there is some change in procedure. These writings are mostly first person exhortation or teaching rather than a second person report. We therefore do not use the second historical approach that we used for the Gospels and Acts. But we still have a historical question to ask. First, we want to know what something from the Epistles of Paul meant for Paul himself and his first audience, and it is only after asking this question that we ask what it means for me or us today. We follow the same procedure for the Epistles of Peter, James, Jude, John, and the books of Hebrews and Revelation. Again, the question of how later generations of believers interpreted passages from these documents is at times important, but it tends to take us beyond the field of New Testament studies.

The church has often recognized the importance of understanding the historical context. One can enter any Christian bookstore and find a number of bible dictionaries that target the layperson. Pastors will often tell their congregations in their sermons the number of soldiers that a Roman centurion commanded or the time of day of the third watch. Many will have made trips to Israel or Turkey and will often have a good grasp of the political situation of the first century. Yet knowledge of the historical context involves much more than an understanding of political issues in the first century. It is necessary to understand such things as the cosmology, the cultural norms, and the social expectations of the people. In short, the New Testament scholar attempts to understand the worldviews of first-century people.

The term "worldviews" is plural because first-century thinkers were not monolithic in their understanding of reality. Just as twentieth-century Christians are composed of various Christian groups who go by various labels such as Evangelical, Protestant, Catholic, Methodist, Lutheran, Episcopal, Baptist, etc., first-century people had numerous groups with which they identified. The family group was of the highest priority, though individuals would identify with various ethnic, regional, religious, occupational, and social groups of various kinds. Thus it is often an overstatement to say such things as, "The Jews in Paul's day believed. . . ." One can only say, "Some Jews in Paul's day believed . . ." or "Certain Jews in Paul's day believed. . . ." Nevertheless, there were many ideas present that large numbers of the population would have embraced.

Using an historical method to try to understand the original meaning of Jesus' teaching, grasp the cultural context of Paul's world, or comprehend the worldviews of the people in the first century is interesting in itself. However, for those of us who seek to apply scripture's teaching to our life, such investigations are a key aspect of a responsible engagement with the Bible. The purpose of historical analysis is to help eliminate arbitrary, purely idiosyncratic, narcissistic, dictatorial, and outright quirky interpretations of the Bible. At the same time, it holds to the belief that the biblical text is a word for us today, just as it has been for generations past.

THE LITERARY QUESTIONS: IT'S ALL ABOUT GENRE

The historical questions that we have explored so far are not the only queries to apply to the New Testament. We also need to ask literary questions about the genre (literary type) and the literary context of a passage. If these two questions, along with that of the question of historical context, can be answered well, many questions regarding Biblical interpretation can be cleared up.

When scripture is studied in a university setting, one of the first questions we ask about any passage is "what is the genre?" The term *genre* is nothing more than a fancy French word that means "kind" or "type" and is usually applied to literature or art. A poem is not the same genre of literature as a telephone listing. Furthermore, there are dozens of types of poems, each having a different genre. Thus, a person trained in literature can easily tell a limerick from a sonnet, though to the untrained eye the differences may not be apparent. Since understanding the genre of a bit of literature tells us a lot about how we should read it, we will immediately know that we will be more likely to find humor in a limerick than a sonnet and that the latter might be more appropriate for Valentine's day than the former.

We make genre decisions every day, though most of the time this is done unconsciously. However, genre recognition is more difficult when the literature we are looking at was written two thousand years ago in a different language by people with a completely different worldview from what we possess today. Even when we are sensitive to the genre, our twenty-first century Western assumptions often cloud our vision. In the study of the New Testament, genre recognition is one of the most important issues in matters of biblical interpretation. For example, since the Gospels speak of the life and teachings of Jesus, we are often inclined to hold the same expectations for the Gospels as we do for modern biographies. But did the writers of the Gospels have the same concerns for such matters as chronology as a contemporary biographer? Since no biography (or Gospel) includes everything the subject says or does, decisions are made about what is important and what can be left out. Does Luke have the same reasons for including certain materials in his Gospel that a biographer will use to determine what to put in her book about George Washington? If we want to respect scripture, we will need to be careful about imposing our assumptions about genre onto the Bible. It is probably not an overstatement to say that some of the biggest errors in biblical interpretation result from failure to recognize genre.

In addition to the cultural difficulty of understanding the various genres within scripture's covers, we have to overcome the problem of "packaging." Because the Bible comes between two covers, we are tempted to see it as a single book, and books generally stick to one single genre from beginning to end. However, once we get between the covers of "The Book," we find that scripture is composed of sixty-six works that are commonly called "books." Only a few of the thirty-nine books of the Old Testament or the twenty-seven books of the New Testament could even remotely be considered books in the usual sense of the word. The Gospels and the book of Acts are the closest things we have to books in the New Testament. The letters of Paul are just that—letters. The same is true of the works that are traditionally called the Catholic Epistles. The last book of the New Testament, the Revelation of John, is the most misunderstood book of all. It, too, is a letter, though the bulk of it is in the genre of apocalypse, a very popular style in the first-century Roman world. Each book of the New Testament is furthermore composed of many genres.

GENRE AND THE LETTERS OF PAUL

Why is genre recognition so important? Let's approach this by looking at Paul's letters as an example. Many students are surprised to learn that Paul didn't decide one day to write the Bible. Instead, he wrote to address current issues in the churches of his day, and he does this by sending letters to a number of individuals and congregations in different places. Some of these Epistles were collected in and later included in what we call the New Testament, but others were not.

Let's unravel the situation at Corinth, a city in the Roman province of Achaia, now southern Greece. We need to discuss the historical setting to gain a grasp on the genre. According to Acts 18:11, Paul preached at Corinth for eighteen months and established a church there. When Paul left Corinth, he moved on to Ephesus (cf. Acts 18:19), located on the other side of the Aegean Sea from Corinth. While in Ephesus, Paul received bad news about immorality in the church in Corinth, and he wrote his first letter to the Corinthians. In this letter Paul told the Corinthian Christians not to associate with immoral persons. This letter is now lost, but we know if its existence from 1 Corinthians 5:9 where Paul makes reference to it. Apparently the Corinthians misunderstood this letter. The Corinthians wrote back to Paul with a series of questions about various problems in the church (cf. 1 Corinthians 7:1). They also sent an oral message by way of servants of a certain Chloe (1 Corinthians 1:11; 16:17). In response, Paul wrote another letter to the Corinthians, (our 1 Corinthians), addressing the various problems. These problems included divisions within the church (1:10–4:21); interfamily marriage (5:1–13); lawsuits between church members (6:1–11); sex with prostitutes (6:12–20); marriage (7); food offered to idols (8:1–11:1); order in worship (11:2–14:40), including covering of heads (11:2–16), the Lord's Supper (11:17–34), and spiritual gifts (12–14); the resurrection of the dead (15); and an offering Paul was collecting for Jerusalem (16:1–4). Paul also sent Timothy by land with oral instructions (1 Corinthians 4:17) for the Corinthian church. Timothy arrived some time after the second letter and, by then, the situation in Corinth had grown worse. Neither the presence of Timothy nor Paul's letter could heal the situation. A group of "missionaries" had arrived, claiming to be "servants of Christ" (2 Corinthians 11:23) and apostles (2 Corinthians 11:5, 13). These "apostles" criticized Paul and made numerous allegations against him. To a large degree they were able to gain the support of the Corinthians. Timothy returned to Ephesus, reporting that his efforts to reclaim the church for Paul were unsuccessful. Paul then made a brief "painful" visit to Corinth (2 Corinthians 2:1–2) and was frustrated in his efforts to regain the church (2 Corinthians 2:5–8; 7:12). He returned to Ephesus in humiliation (12:21). In response Paul wrote a harsh letter "out of much affliction and anguish of heart" (2 Corinthians 2:3–4, 9; 7:8–12). This letter, which is apparently lost (some scholars suggest it is possibly 2 Corinthians 10–13), was hand delivered by Titus to Corinth. The Corinthians recognized their guilt, mourned their wrongs, and wanted to see Paul (2 Corinthians 7:6–7). Paul sent Titus with his fourth letter (our 2 Corinthians), a letter of reconciliation. Finally, Paul visited Corinth to receive an offering for the poor in Jerusalem.

What is the point of this detailed discussion of Paul's relationship with the Corinthians? It simply clarifies the point made earlier. We must first discover what all this meant for Paul and his first audience. Paul is not writing primarily to *us*, whomever that may be. He is writing primarily to the Corinthians. The advice and instruction that he gives to the Corinthian Christians is advice to them first, and may or may not be *directly* applicable to us. When we recognize that Paul is writing as a church planter, pastor, and apostle to a specific situation with unique problems, it reminds us that his letters are not intended to be read as lists of universally valid theological propositions or chapters in a theological textbook. They may nevertheless contain universally valid theological principles, but this can be shown only after we have identified those propositions that are restricted to the specific situations Paul addresses (for example, instructions about women wearing veils and keeping silent in churches).

WHY NEW TESTAMENT STUDY?

Our aim in calling attention to these historical and literary issues in New Testament study is to enable students to provide solid reasons for what they believe regardless of whom they have as a conversation partner. It should be noted that discussions about the historical setting or literary character of a passage are not dependent on a specific religious commitment. Therefore, they provide a substantial chunk of common ground for discussing the meaning of a portion of scripture with those who share our basic religious outlook as well as those who disagree with our positions.

There are more general reasons for why it is important to take New Testament courses in a university. It is impossible to explain Western civilization and American culture without reference to the New Testament. Unless we can explain Western civilization and American culture we can do little to maintain or improve these legacies. New Testament studies not only put us in touch with an important part of our historical and cultural roots, but it also gives us a vantage point from which we can critique, challenge, preserve, and change what we have become.

In addition to the general cultural impact of scripture, the New Testament merits careful study because it shapes our religious beliefs, even if we have never thought about them. At least some of your beliefs about God, sin, salvation, and other basic religious ideas may be rooted in the New Testament. If not, then, the beliefs of people you will encounter certainly have New Testament roots. Biblical studies train us to examine the roots of our beliefs and the beliefs of others. Without such an examination we have no objective grounds for speaking for or against any set or system of beliefs, regardless of how beneficial or detrimental those beliefs may be within the global community.

Unless we find some way to get beyond purely subjective interpretations of scripture, we will be at the mercy of those who use the New Testament to justify awful practices. Unfortunately, history is full of events that illustrate how the New Testament has been used for ill. For example, the Crusades, the Spanish Inquisition, the European-American slave trade, the disenfranchisement of the Native American in the name of Manifest Destiny, the Salem witch hunts, and the Holocaust were all "justified" by appeal to scripture. Even more unfortunate is that these misuses are not limited to a time long ago. In more modern times, the lives of 913 people under the leadership of Jim Jones in Jonestown, Guyana, 82 people under David Koresh in the Branch Davidian compound, and 39 people belonging to the Heavensgate cult all died for beliefs derived from a misapplication of New Testament teachings. Even when misguided interpretations of scripture do not create such overt tragedies, it is probably safe to say that millions throughout history have lived a less satisfying and healthy life than they might have because they misunderstood the message of the New Testament.

NEW TESTAMENT STUDIES AND VOCATION

When students wonder what they can do with training in biblical studies with an emphasis in New Testament, a number of options will come to mind. People with such training have found work as pastors, priests, and ministers in local church congregations; as chaplains in hospitals and prisons; as leaders and staff of parachurch, social service, and nonprofit organizations; as professors and administrators in colleges, universities, and seminaries; and as linguists or archaeologists. Some have also moved into careers that are not as obviously connected with New Testament studies as we might imagine (e.g., artists, musicians, journalists, researchers, media consultants). But what about the majority of students who might take a couple of New Testament courses in college? How do such studies link with callings that seem to have little direct connection?

We took some time above outlining some of the historical and literary background of Paul's letters to the church in Corinth, so we will use an example from one of those letters to illustrate one way investigation of these elements might shape our broader understanding of the Christian's calling. Perhaps the best-known passage from Paul's correspondence with the Corinthians is 1 Corinthians 13:1–13, often called the "Love Chapter." It is frequently used in marriage ceremonies to help us understand what love means in the context of a marriage. However, what happens to our reading of 1 Corinthians 13 when we look at it against the background of the historical and literary questions we have proposed using in our study of the New Testament?

Our quick historical look at the Corinthian church revealed that it was an infant congregation composed of gentile converts. They had no long-standing unified religious tradition to draw from, probably little familiarity with what we now call the Old Testament, and no Christian Bible. As a result of this, they were being torn apart by all sorts of struggles, which Paul is attempting to deal with. Paul cannot come back to Corinth in person but, as we have seen above, knows what the problems are. But what scripture passage should be read at weddings is not one of these pressing problems. So what was Paul thinking about when he wrote 1 Corinthians 13?

This is where our literary investigation kicks in. We know 1 Corinthians is a letter, but Paul also does something in 1 Corinthians that helps us know how to break the letter down into smaller units. A literary approach shows that, at several points, Paul starts sections with the same phrase (usually translated "now concerning"), which indicates that he is addressing a specific problem in Corinth. One of these "now concerning" sections is 1 Corinthians 12–14, which tells us that 1 Corinthians 13 should be read in the context of the chapters on either side of it. What we find in 1 Corinthians 12 and 14 is a pitched battle within the church over spiritual gifts.

At the risk of oversimplifying this section of the Bible, the Corinthians are at each other's throats about the status and priority of certain spiritual gifts, and tragically it appears that some within the congregation view their particular gifts as a sign of their spiritual superiority over others. 1 Corinthians 13 is part of Paul's response to this. In this context, one of the messages he wants to send is that no matter how impressive our gifts or functions within the church, if we use them in ways that are arrogant, unkind, self-ish, or rude (1 Corinthians 13:4–5—i.e., in unloving ways), they are all worthless.

What does all this mean for a Christian in the workplace? We all want to feel that what we do is important and honored. This need can be twisted into a situation where we elevate our skills and responsibilities (or demean the skills and responsibilities of others) in prideful ways. In the workplace, the pecking order embedded in the hierarchical structure can lure us into thinking that demeaning attitudes toward those we consider below us is acceptable. However, Paul would remind us that if we use the gifts and roles God gives us in unloving ways, while we might not suffer within the corporate structure, by God's measure we are as annoying as "a noisy gong or a clanging cymbal" (1 Corinthians 13:1). In short, then, the "Love Chapter" stands as God's challenge to the customary measures of what is important in the workplace (and all too often in the church).

Do these historical and literary considerations mean, then, that we should not use 1 Corinthians 13 in a wedding ceremony? Not at all. But the context also reminds us that it would be a good idea for spouses to reread this chapter when facing difficult situations later in the marriage, because it talks about the type of love that involves hard decisions. During the wedding, we don't have to work at love. The feelings come pretty naturally. However, in a marriage, or in the workplace, our insecurity, pride, and self-ishness will come to the surface time after time, and this chapter reminds us that love is a choice that God demands against the strong pressures to act in unloving ways. God's way of determining the "greatest" has little to do with one's status, competencies, the size of paychecks, or other things that are temporary. Instead, God measures in terms of what lasts forever—love (1 Corinthians 13:13).

7

CHURCH HISTORY: SURROUNDED BY A GREAT CLOUD OF WITNESSES

Dennis Okholm

In 1969 Ray Bakke became pastor of a small inner-city Chicago church while simultaneously teaching and studying at McCormick Theological Seminary. In his book *A Theology as Big as the City*, he relates an anecdote about a Presbyterian pastor, John Fry, who was greatly admired on the seminary campus. Trained in the Marines and at Princeton Seminary, he had become an "antiestablishment pro-urban pastor" during the rollicking era of civil rights and Vietnam. In the lunchroom a student asked what it took to be a really "with it" pastor. After stunning the students with his insistence that they had no business in the ministry unless they could read Hebrew and translate any passage in the Greek New Testament, he concluded with his rationale, "If you can't tell me where the church has been, you have no business telling me where it ought to go." Never having forgotten those words and now a seasoned urban minister, Bakke clearly states the principle, "the further one goes into the avant-garde frontier of creative ministry, the more important it becomes that we be deeply rooted in the biblical, theological, and historical tradition. We need deep roots to survive in urban ministry."[1] Indeed, we need deep roots to survive in *any* Christian ministry.

What a contrast to the independent Fundamentalist church in Milwaukee where I was assistant pastor right after I graduated from Wheaton College. I was suspect (and on six-month probation) from the beginning, since I, like the pastor's daughters, had pursued a college degree from a "liberal" institution. I lasted only two months beyond my probation period, but the experience taught me what I *needed* to learn about ministry, the history of the church, and biblical exegesis as I headed off for seminary to pursue a couple master's degrees. Unfortunately, folks in the church did not share my passion to learn more. They asked, "Why do you need to get more education? You've already been to college!" For whatever reason, the people I pastored did not appreciate the value of an educated ministry. I was saddened when I heard that a year after my departure they had dismissed their pastor of seventeen years for, among other things, trying to educate the congregation about religions with which Christianity is in competition and when I learned that a few years later the church had splintered apart and dissolved.

I had to venture well into the first year of my seminary education before I began to understand how I might have been part of the solution more than part of the problem in what was really a dysfunctional church family. In fact, that is really what the Christian church is: a family with a rich heritage that begins with Adam and Eve (at least, according to John Calvin) and continues through millennia of dysfunction and function to the present moment.

THE HISTORY OF A FAMILY

I grew up hearing stories about my relatives on both sides of the family. My maternal grandmother always insisted that we were direct descendants of a Pennsylvania signatory of the U. S. Constitution. After spending a day digging through the Lancaster and Reading archives I discovered that the signatory in question had no male heirs. The truth hurt, but the myth was exposed. On my paternal side I grew up hearing stories about how my grandfather had immigrated to the United States from Denmark and homesteaded in Nevada and, later, northern California. That piece of information helps to explain why I grew up in California and not Florida. And that same grandfather is, in part, responsible for my early religious upbringing in strict Pentecostalism—a tradition that my father embraced but my uncle rejected by leaving home at sixteen. My cousins and I are all "Okholms," but the brothers' responses to their father's faith goes far to help me understand my cousins' spiritual quests in New Age spiritualities while I became more entrenched in the Christian faith. The two brothers did have a celebration shortly after my grandfather died when they discovered they had a half-brother in Denmark about whom they knew nothing. Apparently grandfather's strict faith was as vulnerable as King David's.

In fact, just as the oral traditions about my ancestors circulate among family members and help to articulate a heritage that reinforces (and cautions against) a way of thinking, acting, and viewing the world, so David and his peers were encouraged to remember their history in order to think, act, and view the world as God's chosen people. Listen to the prologue (Verses 1–8) of Psalm 78's recitation of Israel's history:

Give ear, O my people, to my teaching; incline your ears to the words of my mouth. I will open my mouth in a parable; I will utter dark sayings from of old, things that we have heard and known, that our ancestors have told us. We will not hide them from their children; we will tell to the coming generation the glorious deeds of the Lord and his might and the wonders that he has done.

He established a decree in Jacob and appointed a law in Israel, which he commanded our ancestors to teach to their children; that the next generation might know them, the children yet unborn, and rise up and tell them to their children, so that they should set their hope in God, and not forget the works of God, but keep his commandments; and that they should not be like their ancestors, a stubborn and rebellious generation, a generation whose heart was not steadfast, whose spirit was not faithful to God.

This is what the discipline of "church history" is all about: to keep the heritage alive by hearing the stories of Christian ancestors in order to know how to think and act and view the world as people who go by the family name "Christian." From the time church kids are in the nursery they should be meeting other members of the family—both dead and alive—seeing their pictures (though Ulrich Zwingli's might scare them until they're a little older), hearing their stories (like the heroic stand taken by Latimer and Ridley as they were burned at the stake for their faith), observing their feast days (as we do "holy days" commemorating national heroes like Martin Luther King Jr.), and celebrating their achievements (such as the preservation of Western civilization and literature during what was known as the Dark Ages). Pasted into the Christian family album are snapshots of generations past that have communicated to the present generation certain Christian traits, behaviors, and beliefs. The stories and snapshots conjure up remorse, embarrassment, joy, pride, satisfaction, longing, wonder, and a host of other conflicted emotions.

Chances are that these church kids will not begin in just *any* nursery, but in a *particular* nursery—that is, Baptist or Lutheran or Catholic or Nazarene or Greek Orthodox. In other words, we Christians represent a large extended family with various branches that are connected to brothers and sisters whose features we share and to relatives who are from so far away and so long ago that "six degrees of separation" doesn't even come close. Still, we all belong to the same family tree, sharing some of the same heritage, detecting some commonalities, and distinguished by peculiarities that set one branch off from another. Knowing how the tree has grown helps us to understand why Christians act or see things differently.

Just as I have learned what it means to be an Okholm descended from one of two brothers, so we learn much about ourselves when we look at our varied past. We find out what it means to be on our particular side of the family tree, discover how our attitudes and behavior differ from those that characterize other sides of the family tree, and learn how we can do better in the future. In other words, we can have a better understanding of who we are and where we fit in the Christian story.

Sometimes we hear stories about adopted children who seek out their birth parents. They often do it to better understand who they are, why they are who they are, and how they can provide their children with a sense of identity and purpose that goes beyond an untethered adolescence. In the same way and for similar reasons, Christians ought to be interested in their own past history. Indeed, Christians are like an "old money" family—heirs of a legacy that has borne interest over the centuries. The "faith once delivered to the saints" (Jude 3) has been invested in those who followed, has accrued interest as more people joined the family, and has been more deeply understood and richly expressed. But to claim the legacy that is ours as Christian descendants, we must be very intentional about finding out what the legacy involves and how we can participate in it now. That is why an academic discipline like church history is so important for the church. That is why Pastor John Fry said what he did to those seminary students.

WHAT IS THE STUDY OF HISTORY, AND WHY IS IT IMPORTANT?

Church history focuses on the institution of the church—how it has grown and split, how it is governed, how events and persons are related to one another, and so forth. Essentially, it is a branch of world history—appropriate for Christians who believe that God has entered into our world in Jesus Christ (whose body is now the church). And just as we cultivate good U.S. citizens by teaching them the history of the United States, so we cultivate good citizens of a particular church by teaching them the history of their denomination or congregation and how it relates to the histories of other Christian groups.

A discipline related to church history is historical theology. While church history is more focused on institutions, persons, and events, historical theology is a subcategory of the history of ideas. That is, it deals with the sources of Christian traditions and the development of ideas within the history of the Christian church. For instance, it helps us to understand the difference between a Roman Catholic understanding of the Lord's Supper and that of a Baptist . . . and perhaps why those differences came into play. Historians of theology also study the ideas of individuals (like Augustine and Luther and the relation of their understandings of justification, for example), of movements (such as the Worldwide Church of God), and of schools of theology (a good example of which is the Alexandrians and the Antiochenes who debated how Jesus Christ could be both human and divine at the same time). Historical theologians who are worth their salt always keep the church's history in the background, especially when studying something like the origins of Anglican theology. And they remind themselves that they engage in this study within the company of believers and for the sake of the church. After all, historical theologians are members of the very church whose ideas they are studying. There is something in it for them.

Now, when I entered college the first courses I took were the two required in the history of civilization. It wasn't because the topic caused me to salivate every time I thought about it. I took the two courses in eight weeks of summer school before my freshman year in order to get them out of the way. For four hours each day I sat in a dreary basement classroom with three other students while we listened to a lecture that followed a daily quiz on the incredibly boring textbook that provided an antidote to insomnia. But in my last year of college I took a class called Historical Theology: Reformation to Kant. To use the lingo of the times, I got turned on. For the first time I realized that history was not simply a collection of facts and dates to be memorized for the exam. It also involved the interaction of ideas of real people facing issues of, well, historic proportions. And they were ideas that had consequences.

For example, in the late Middle Ages a school of thought called Nominalism challenged another school of thought called Realism. The latter school (represented by folks like Thomas Aquinas) believed, among other things, that emperors and princes and bishops and priests ruled because that is *really* the way that things are in the universe as God has established it. The former school (represented by folks like William of Occam) objected: Such people rule because humans arbitrarily decided that that is the way they wanted to organize their lives. (A good way to think of the dispute is to ask yourself whether all animals designated "cats" are so designated because there is something about "catness" that all such animals have or because we have just decided that certain animals should have the name (*nomina*) "cats" and other animals should be named "dogs.") The Nominalist view was a threat to the established order, because people might decide that there are other ways to govern themselves, such as through the decisions of councils that were more representative of the people. Add to this the idea that God's grace is only available to people through this God-ordained order, and you can see why the reformer Martin Luther, who was influenced by a popular brand of Nominalism, was seen as such a threat to the powers that be at the beginning of the Protestant Reformation.

Such ideas have consequences for our lives, even today. For example, consider the difference between a monarch who rules because God ordains it and a democracy that insists the people make their own decisions about who rules and how. The difference might be compared to the current debate about marriage: Is it an institution established by God that only involves a man and a woman (like the Realists might insist), or is it an institution designating various kinds of sexual relationships and arbitrarily labeled "marriage" by folks in a democratic society (like the Nominalists might insist)?

So church history and historical theology are not merely about dates. Dates are important as pegs to orient you in the story (e.g., this came before that). In fact, if you knew the significance for church history of the years 312, 325, 451, 800, 1054, and 1517, you'd be well on your way to understanding the plot line of the church's history and how we ended up with three major branches of the Christian church (Roman Catholic, Eastern Orthodox, and Protestant). Dates are just tools by which we can relate events to one another. (If nothing else it will help you avoid asking embarrassing questions like the one a student posed in one of my classes: "Did Descartes come before or after Jesus?")

Nor is church history merely about bare facts (as it seemed when I sat in that dreary basement over thirty years ago). There is always a relationship between data and interpretation, particularly when we are trying to account for data that happened centuries ago. A good example of this occurred when a Princeton Seminary librarian was explaining to doctoral students and interested professors the new computerized catalog that was replacing the drawers and drawers of cards. (This is ancient history for some of you.) The librarian demonstrated how we could locate books on a subject or cross list subjects to refine our search further. All was clear until a professor visiting from the United Kingdom posed a query no one had considered. He asked, "If I want to search for books about the conflict between England and her North American colonies in the late eighteenth century, do I ask for books on the American Revolution or the rebellion of the colonies?"

We can find the same thing as we study church history. For instance, in the aftermath of Luther's protest Rome engaged in some serious house cleaning (a bit too late for some people), attending to her own reforms in doctrine and church practice. Some refer to this as the "Counter Reformation," while others refer to this as the "Catholic Reformation." The first places the event in the context of the Lutheran protest and has some negative connotations, while the latter stands in its own right and has a more positive tone. Furthermore, interpreting what was going on at that time in the debates about the doctrine of justification is not as clear as once thought. Merely to state that Luther was arguing for justification by faith over against a Roman Catholic doctrine of salvation by works is to misconstrue the argument. It's more complicated than that. The church historian helps us to see that, in part, Lutherans and Catholics were arguing about the correct understanding of justification in the teaching of Augustine, while, at the same time, they probably did not even understand each other.

TAKING CARE TO GET HISTORY RIGHT

So some cautions are in order as we approach a study of the Christian church's history and its ideas, but they are cautions that make the study all that much more interesting.

First, the way the church historian interprets the data will depend to some degree on the social location and upbringing of the historian. In other words, a white European will probably have a different understanding of the church's history than a black African. In fact, even in the United States an African American will have a very different assessment of the history of Fundamentalism and American evangelicalism than a white evangelical.[2]

Second, the way the church historian interprets the data will depend to some degree on what is singled out or what is left out, along with interpretive keys that unlock the meaning of history. Some might focus on the Protestant Reformation and, through that event, read with pessimism the preceding fifteen hundred years. In fact, many evangelical Protestants skip from Paul to Luther, thinking that nothing significant happened in-between. But a study of Luther himself quickly demonstrates that he cannot be understood apart from the influence of years spent in an Augustinian monastery, let alone from the theology of the schools in the Middle Ages against which he reacted.

During the last two millennia Christian theologians and church historians have often distorted the church's history for pragmatic or utilitarian purposes. For example, in the fifth century some Romans charged that Christianity had undermined the social order and was responsible for the decline of the Roman Empire. In response, Augustine wrote *The City of*

God as an apology (or defense) to demonstrate to the Romans that when you trace world history from its beginning there have always been two societies that have fought against each other—the society of those for whom the love of God is central (the "City of God") and the society of those for whom the love of the human self is central (the "City of Man"); and, if anything, Rome's demise, Augustine argued, is due to the sin of the latter society, not to the Christian church, which champions the former society. In a similar way, a thousand years later during the Reformation, Heinrich Bullinger, the successor of John Calvin in Geneva, wrote "The Old Faith" to prove that the Protestant Reformers had not left the church. In fact, they were in line with the proclaimers of the Gospel since it was first announced in Genesis 3:15, while the Roman church had been the one to veer from the old faith.

Third, the way the church historian interprets the data will depend to some degree on the kinds of questions posed. A biblical scholar might ask what clues there are in the biblical text to indicate that Jesus is God. A systematic theologian might ask how we should properly understand the incarnation of God in Christ. But the church historian and the historical theologian will investigate the various early attempts to explain what it meant for Christians to say "the word became flesh," trace the process by which schools of thought fought with each other (involving some dirty politics and alliances with secular political leaders), and interpret the "Definition of Chalcedon" that was hammered out as a result of this five-century debate—a creedal statement that has grounded all Christian churches in their understanding of who Jesus Christ is.

WHY STUDY CHURCH HISTORY?

So far we have suggested that the motivation for studying church history is not unlike that of investigating our family heritage, that church history involves more than memorizing dates, and that the church member who studies the history of the church needs to be aware of the perspective from which he is looking back. Along the way we have implied some reasons why it is important for church folks to appreciate the disciplines of church history and historical theology. Now it is appropriate to be more specific about those reasons.

First, studying church history helps us to make sense of the past. We make connections between persons and events and movements. I remember the time that my wife, who is a Christian education director, walked by a

Sunday school classroom one Saturday and saw one of her teachers preparing for a lesson with a look of exasperation. My wife discovered that the teacher was frustrated because she couldn't make sense of the lesson. So they sat down together and looked at how the story for the next day fit into the whole biblical story. The light went on, confusion melted away, and the teacher felt confident about her grasp of what she was to teach the children. In the same way we might be able to make better sense of something like the beginnings of Protestant liberalism with Friedrich Schleiermacher's publication of *Speeches on Religion to Its Cultured Despisers* in 1799. If we understand the context in which he wrote this book we soon realize that Protestant liberalism did not arise in order to undermine the Christian faith, but to establish it more firmly in the face of attacks from various quarters.

Second, studying church history helps us to put the present in perspective. As members of a particular denomination or church, who are we, how did we get to be who we are, how do we differ from others, and what is the significance of what we are doing now? C. S. Lewis made this point when he suggested that ignorance of the past is a bit like entering into a conversation late:

> If you join at eleven o'clock a conversation which began at eight you will often not see the real bearing of what is said. Remarks which seem to you very ordinary will produce laughter or irritation and you will not see why—the reason, of course, being that the earlier stages of the conversation have given them a special point.[3]

For instance, a secular magazine recently reported that in the last few years American evangelicals have been one of Israel's most ardent supporters. But a study of John Nelson Darby and the history of dispensationalism (a teaching about the end times that is fictionalized in the *Left Behind* series) reveals that American evangelicals and their predecessors have been Israel's most ardent supporters even when the modern nation state was just a gleam in the eyes of Jews scattered throughout the world. In fact, those who equate the *Left Behind* series with biblical teaching about the last days would do well to heed the words of church historian Justo González, who helps us to understand the significance of the point we are making here:

> Without understanding that past, we are unable to understand ourselves, for in a sense the past still lives in us and influences who we are and how we understand the Christian message. . . . The notion that we read the New Testament exactly as the early Christians did, without any weight of tradition coloring our interpretation, is an illusion. It is also a

dangerous illusion, for it tends to absolutize our interpretation, confusing it with the word of God.[4]

Third, studying church history gives us guidance for the future. By studying the past we can avoid repeating mistakes. We can be a bit calmer, even in the midst of church fights, confident that all is not lost and that the church somehow continues to survive and even thrive in the aftermath of conflict. Contrarily, we might become appropriately alarmed when we are tempted to kick back, especially as we realize some of the consequences of past events in the life of the church. In other words, the past provides us with a map drawn by folks who have already been there and done that. We have road signs we can trust, because folks have already traveled around the corner we are nearing, and they know how we should approach the turn and at what speed. Again, Lewis made this point so well as he recommended reading old books in order to learn from the past:

> Not, of course, that there is any magic about the past. People were no cleverer then than they are now; they made as many mistakes as we. But not the *same* mistakes. They will not flatter us in the errors we are already committing; and their own errors, being now open and palpable, will not endanger us. Two heads are better than one, not because either is infallible, but because they are unlikely to go wrong in the same direction. To be sure, the old books of the future would be just as good a corrective as the books of the past, but unfortunately we cannot get at them.[5]

In the process, we might redraw the map a bit more accurately to benefit those who travel the same road after us.

Just as my family had to deal with the revelations of my grandfather's past dalliances, a good example of guiding the church based on learning of embarrassing and even horrible events in the church's past occurred during my years teaching at Wheaton College. Since I taught church history, some students asked me to write an essay for the student paper on the history of the Crusades. They were questioning the wisdom of Wheaton's mascot— the Crusaders. Letters to the editor followed, along with vigorous campus debate. Finally, when the college president reviewed the church's history during the twelfth and thirteenth centuries, he concluded that it was inappropriate to continue using Crusaders as a mascot in connection with a Christian school. (Many mission agencies made this decision long ago, particularly if they were active in Europe or the Middle East, since folks in those parts of the world have long memories of the atrocities that were committed in the name of Christ.) The mascot name was changed, and we avoided perpetuating an error the church had made by learning lessons for our future from our Christian family's past.

Fourth, studying church history and historical theology helps us to understand the Christian faith better in community with others "whose rest is won," as that great hymn "The Church's One Foundation" puts it. (By the way, knowing the history of the church conflict that led Samuel John Stone to write this hymn will make those who sing appreciate it all the more . . . and perhaps sing it with more gusto!) The apostle Paul prays for the church in Ephesians 3:14–19 that they might come to know the multidimensional reality of God (the length, depth, breadth, and width) "with *all* the saints." In other words, we are part of one gigantic Bible study that includes church members such as Athanasius, Augustine, Anselm, and Aquinas (and we haven't even moved beyond the A's yet!). It includes Hildegard, Teresa, Luther, Calvin, Wesley, Barth, and, of course, people in your local church whom you can see. As Karl Barth put it, we don't so much study Augustine as become *fellow students* with Augustine.[6] Those in the past left us their reflections on the biblical text and their understanding of Christian belief and practice. They might not sit in our living rooms along with the rest of our covenant group, but their books sit on our shelves, and as we read their reflections on the Bible and Christianity, we can learn from them and even debate with them.

At this point we need to take a slight detour to recommend the reading of "old" books. If we are going to take church history and historical theology seriously, we really must read books not often found in the local Christian bookstore. But we have become *chronocentric*: We don't like to venture out past our present, and we feel comfortable living exclusively in the neighborhood of our contemporaries. C. S. Lewis helps us to understand this bias against the "old" books.[7]

For one thing, we think that the latest is best. Many conservative Christians would not dream of entertaining the slightest Darwinian thought, yet this belief that the "latest is best" is precisely an evolutionary bias that is, at the same time, pretentious. And if we *are* better than those who have come before us, it is probably because we stand on their shoulders.

For another thing, we think that what is older is more difficult to read. Yet many in the past were great precisely because they were easier to understand. Anyone who has read Plato, for instance, knows that he is far easier to understand than books written by our contemporaries *about* Plato. Yet, how many of us who want to know what Plato said often turn first to the book about him rather than to the dialogue written by him? I have found this especially true with regard to John Calvin. His *Institutes of the Christian Religion* is arguably the greatest work produced in the Protestant Reformation. When my students read his book they are amazed to find a pastor-theologian who doesn't sound quite like some of the Calvinists who are popular authors today—writers who often out-Calvin Calvin and distort his more humble theological musings in the process.

So we should take Lewis's advice: Read one old book for every two new ones.

A fifth reason for studying church history is based on the fact that our only access to the Gospel of Jesus Christ is *through* history. We *must* admit this because we are people of the incarnation: God comes to us *in* history *using* human language. Again, González puts it so well:

> From its very beginning, the Christian message was grafted onto human history. . . . Without that story, it is impossible to know that [i.e., God's] revelation. . . . It is a history of the deeds of the Spirit in and through the men and women who have gone before us in the faith. . . . The history of those deeds through sinners such as us. . . . Through those sinners and that church—and only through them—the biblical message has come to us.[8]

When studying church history it's good to remember that we not only have access to the Gospel through history because God the Son *has* come to us, but also because God the Spirit *continues* to work in the church and in the world. Time and again I am amazed how the Holy Spirit has guided the church through some of its worst times to accomplish God's kingdom purposes. For instance, if you read the story of how Cyril of Alexandria railroaded his agenda against the Antiochenes (a competing church center in the early church's life) in a dastardly game of church politics, you might decide that nothing good can come of it. But read on! You will discover that the church was able to right the wrongs and even use Cyril's ideas twenty years later to help formulate the orthodox teaching of the human and divine natures in the one person of Jesus Christ. Reading about such episodes in the church's history strengthens a Christian's confidence that God has not been inactive since the Spirit inspired the writers of scripture, but has been actively guiding Christ's church as Lord.[9]

Finally, we study church history and historical theology to develop our spiritual lives. I'll never forget the experience in that historical theology course in college when I watched the old black-and-white movie of Martin Luther's life and the events of the Reformation. (Then it was on 16 mm film. Now I own it on a DVD. History marches on!) I was inspired as I witnessed the courage of that renegade monk, and I remember thinking, "I want to be like him!" Since that initiation into the history of the church and its theologies, I have been inspired (and sometimes frightened or ashamed) by the characters and events that I have studied.

UNDERSTANDING VOCATION

In fact, this initial foray into historical studies helped me to understand better the role that Christians like myself are to play in society—a role that is linked to the concept of vocation (from the Latin root *vocatio* and a word we often associate with "calling").

Studying the church's history and its thinkers helps a modern-day Christian to understand that there is not simply one way for the church to relate to the culture in which it exists. H. Richard Niebuhr's classic study *Christ and Culture* surveyed twenty centuries of church history and came up with five ways in which Christians have typically responded to the culture that surrounds them. One extreme was withdrawal from the culture. I saw my early Pentecostal and Baptist experience in a new light when I read Niebuhr's account of this "Christ against Culture" position held by Tertullian in the third century and by monks in the Middle Ages. It explained why our church youth group huddled in a banquet room for a Christian formal (and "safe") dating experience on the same night that all of our "pagan" public school classmates went dancing at the Senior Prom. And it might help us to understand why some sense a call to teach in a Christian private (and "safe") school instead of in a public institution that is thought to be a breeding house for the Enemy's "dangerous" ideas.

The other extreme was the church dominating the culture, drawing especially on the history of medieval Christendom's "Christ above Culture" posture; this helps me to put into perspective such contemporary movements as the religious right in the United States. Instead of withdrawing into private educational institutions, those Christians who advocate the dominating stance might hear God's call to run for the school board or devote themselves to a full-time career in politics in order to steer public education in a Christian direction.

On a personal level Niebuhr's models affect our concept of vocation. Christians are called by Christ to serve the King wherever and whenever he calls (what Calvin called the "sentry post" to which God assigns each of us). One of the ways that Christians have understood their vocation is similar to the separatist extreme among Niebuhr's categories. During the church's early and medieval history there arose a distinction between the higher calling of a life of contemplation and the inferior calling of a life of action. In the former category were folks like monks and priests, and it was these in the "higher life" who were the "called"—the ones with a vocation. As this developed these who followed the higher way could even act as spiritual substitutes for those who led the active life of farming, smithing, or the like, saying prayers and conducting spiritual services on their behalf.

This dualism even creeps into modern evangelical concepts of Christian vocation, such that, even though Paul makes clear in Ephesians that we are *all* ministers, we often use the term to refer only to pastors in the church. But a survey of Reformation history enables us to see that Protestants like Martin Luther rejected such a dualism and declared that *all* tasks done out of faith and to the glory of God were callings or vocations:

> The works of monks and priests, however holy and arduous they be, do not differ one whit in the sight of God from the works of the rustic laborer in the field or the woman going about her household tasks, but that all works are measured before God by faith alone. . . . Indeed, the menial housework of a manservant or maidservant is often more acceptable to God than all the fastings and other works of a monk or priest, because the monk or priest lacks faith.[10]

This historical reminder might help us to avoid some of the hypocrisy and pretension of modern pastors and Christian celebrities and appreciate even more the dignity of the work done by the church janitor or a business manager. And it will also reinforce the point we have already made—namely, that ideas have consequences, for church historians have made the case that the Protestant understanding of vocation partially accounts for the rise and growth of modern capitalism. If ordinary tasks such as manual labor and wise investments are given the dignity of calling, then hard work and shrewd fiscal practices are reinforced. For instance, a mutual fund manager might oversee investments that maximize returns for a Christian ministry or for investors who are enabled to make positive contributions to society; the manager might even set up funds that encourage individuals and companies to invest their money in socially responsible enterprises, avoiding stocks that do directly benefit society or that work against kingdom values such as the just treatment of all human beings.

But we can also learn from our survey of church history that vocation is not simply synonymous with "job" when a job is defined by the society's dictates.[11] When work for work's sake takes on sacred dimensions then we end up with an idolatrous concept of vocation, exemplified in the words of Calvin Coolidge ("The man who builds a factory builds a temple. The man who works there worships there.") and Henry Ford ("Work is the salvation of the human race, morally, physically, socially.").[12] When we so secularize the concept of vocation then our work can even get in the way of serving God! We might find ourselves becoming so immersed in and devoted to our work that our job takes center stage and Jesus becomes peripheral. We might even put such emphasis on doing service for God that we lose sight of the one for whom we do it. We need to make sure that we are not working to prove our own significance, to justify our own existence, or to have a memorial established in our name. As Os Guinness assures us, "The call of God blocks the path of all such deeply human tendencies. We are not primarily called to do something or go somewhere; we are called to someone."[13]

A study of the church's past conceptions of vocation can help us, then, to recover a healthy sense of call for *all* Christians. For the Christian family in the United States it also helps to study the church's progress as it made its way across the Western frontier by means of revivalists who called for quick decisions for Christ, since the evangelized might not be alive the next day. This helps to explain, perhaps, why many American evangelicals believe that the central message of the Gospel is to "get saved so that you can go to heaven," when the central message of Jesus in the Gospels was all about entering and serving the kingdom. This self-understanding out of our past helps us recover an even more robust sense of vocation, since what Christ calls us to is not merely eternal "fire insurance," but kingdom work regardless of our station in life. Whether preaching on city sidewalks or cleaning toilets or conducting research to cure cancer, if the Christian is called to the task it's all service for the kingdom. In fact, as Jesus reminded us, the servant of the servants is the greatest in the kingdom (Mark 10:43–44), and the good news is that *anyone* can qualify. Studying the history of the Christian family provides us with a long walk down a hallway gallery filled with the portraits of saints who teach us over and over the lesson that Christ taught.

NOTES

1. Ray Bakke, *A Theology as Big as the City* (Downers Grove, IL: InterVarsity Press, 1997), 26–27.

2. For instance, see Ronald C. Potter, "Race, Theological Discourse and the Continuing American Dilemma," in *Theology in Black and White: Theological Resources for Racial Reconciliation*, ed. Dennis Okholm (Downers Grove, IL: InterVarsity Press, 1997), 27–36.

3. C. S. Lewis, introduction to *On the Incarnation of the Word* (Crestwood, NY: St. Vladimir's Seminary Press, 1975), 4.

4. Justo González, *The Story of Christianity* (San Francisco: HarperSanFrancisco, 1984), xvii

5. Lewis, introduction to *On the Incarnation of the Word*, 5.

6. Karl Barth, *An Introduction to Evangelical Theology* (Grand Rapids, MI: William B. Eerdmans, 2000), 4–6.

7. See Lewis, introduction to *On the Incarnation of the Word*, 7–8.

8. Gonzalez, *The Story of Christianity*, xv–xvi.

9. A great way to read church history is to read it as the story of the Holy Spirit's work in Charles Williams's *The Descent of the Dove* (Vancouver, British Columbia: Regent College Publishing, 2001).

10. Martin Luther, "The Babylonian Captivity of the Church," quoted in Os Guinness, *The Call* (Nashville, TN: Word Publishing, 1998), 34.

11. See Guinness, *The Call*, chapters 4 and 5 for his historical treatment of what he calls the Catholic and Protestant distortions of the Christian concept of vocation.

12. Quoted in Guinness, *The Call*, 41.

13. Guinness, *The Call*, 43.

8

SYSTEMATIC THEOLOGY: THEOLOGY IN, FOR, AND FROM THE CHURCH

Heather Ann Ackley

The preceding chapters have explored the perceived divide between church and academy in relation to philosophy, ethics, biblical interpretation, and church history. Church and academy have also debated over doctrine: who creates it, who interprets it, and what it means. Since the Protestant Reformation, some Christian churches have even wondered if they needed any explicit doctrine at all. These questions are the concern of systematic theology.

FIRST VERY BASIC QUESTION: WHAT IS SYSTEMATIC THEOLOGY?

Systematic theology is the study of the beliefs and values that Christians have agreed upon as essential to Christian faith and life since the earliest centuries of the church. A systematic theologian studies the Bible, church history, and general revelation (or the way God is revealed through creation and everyday experience) to understand all the implications of what it means to be a Christian. One of systematic theology's most important contributions is its exploration of how different aspects of the Christian faith fit together. This is where the "systematic" in systematic theology comes from. When a systematic theologian discovers an apparent conflict between core Christian teachings and values, that is when she really gets to work. A theologian's job at that point is to go back to the sources of Christian teaching to try to improve her understanding, maybe even in a way that can benefit the whole church.

For example, until the late nineteenth century, some Christians in Europe and the United States enslaved others and saw no apparent conflict between this behavior and biblical teaching. Therefore, the movement to abolish slavery had to work hard to demonstrate that treating other human beings as slaves was inconsistent with biblical teaching and with the historical application of those teachings in mutually agreed upon core Christian values about human nature and relationships. This is the work of systematic theology.

Christians today sometimes think of systematic theology as an exclusively academic discipline, so abstract that it is of little importance to lay Christians and congregations. This perception is somewhat ironic since the first theologians were clearly servants of the church—pastors, bishops, and councils of church leaders—who developed Christian doctrines specifically to address disputes within and between congregations over matters of faith, practice and biblical interpretation. Today, systematic theologians are less often pastors and bishops than professional scholars: Even those systematic theologians who are ordained to ministry tend to focus their professional teaching efforts primarily in a university or seminary setting rather than in a congregation. To whatever extent churches today reject the academic discipline of systematic theology as irrelevant, they may be (even unknowingly) raising an issue that should concern academic theologians. Perhaps we have strayed from our roots as a pastoral discipline that addresses the immediate needs and questions of the church.

SECOND VERY BASIC QUESTION: WHAT DOES SYSTEMATIC THEOLOGY ADDRESS?

Why practice systematic theology at all? This is a very real question that today's churches may direct toward universities and seminaries. Systematic theology is important because it helps us to answer questions that have divided churches and helps us to avoid and respond to false teachings. (False teachings misrepresent Christianity by incorrectly understanding or applying scriptures and historically agreed-upon Christian truths.) For example, in the third and fourth centuries, some Christians became confused about the relationship between God and Jesus Christ. Christian scriptures and apostolic teaching clearly proclaimed that Jesus Christ was the son of God. However, early Christians weren't entirely sure what this meant. In a human father-son relationship, the father comes first in time and in authority. Some

Christians reasoned that this must mean that God likewise existed before Jesus Christ and had authority over him.

A teacher named Arius was famous for popularizing this view, which enough Christians found convincing that a worldwide convention of church leaders had to be organized to think about this problem theologically. They had to study scriptures, pray for the guidance of the Holy Spirit, use their God-given reason to reflect on the problem, and seek consensus with one another about this, because the Christian church was being torn apart by those who accepted Arius's teaching and those who argued against it as unbiblical and unreasonable. Finally, this group of church leaders, the Council of Nicea, agreed on the doctrine that Christians still agree upon today—that God and Jesus Christ are essentially one, not two. Christians agreed that Jesus Christ was not a created being, like we are, but is rather the one "by whom all things were made." By agreeing upon these theological assertions, early Christian leaders were able to explain something very important about what Christians believe about God and Jesus Christ in a way that prevented further spread of a false teaching that was dividing the church.

Today, we still approach theological reflection in the same way as these early church leaders. The academic study of systematic theology is really a way of teaching a consistent method of theological reflection. To practice this method as well as possible, a foundation in biblical studies, church history, philosophy, and practical theology is necessary. This is because systematic theology draws on a variety of resources to answer debates about Christian belief and practice.

Chief among these resources is the Bible. A theological statement first and foremost must be consistent with biblical teaching to be considered a theologically sound Christian statement. However, since Christians have been known to debate the meaning, interpretation, and application of biblical texts, other sources sometimes prove important in discerning between various theological options. For example, the study of theology gives consideration to the historical Christian tradition so that we can learn how Christians have resolved these debates in the past and what Christians through the ages have agreed is essential to the Christian faith (such as the unity of God and Jesus Christ). Systematic theologians also benefit from applying philosophical reasoning to the study of Christian doctrines. While some historical truths of the Christian tradition are accepted on faith and defy logic (for example, that Jesus Christ is fully human and fully divine), it may help us when explaining our faith to others to avoid contradicting ourselves.

Perhaps not all systematic theologians agree upon the importance of practical theology to their discipline, but as stated earlier, this is a matter where both the church and also the historical origins of doctrine and theology may provide a helpful challenge to the academy. Augustine of Hippo, Martin Luther, John Calvin, John Wesley, Dietrich Bonhoeffer, and Martin Luther King Jr. are among the many influential Christians who have contributed both to the academic study of theology and to the life of the church as pastoral leaders. In fact, each of them explicitly drew from their pastoral experiences to write theological work that helped them to address their churches' needs. Those who practice theological reflection in the Wesleyan tradition tend to be quite explicit about the consideration of the way that experience raises certain theological questions and ideas, though the Bible remains the authoritative source for any theological response to those questions.

Just as systematic theology draws on the other disciplines taught in an undergraduate Christian university or seminary, the other disciplines draw and build on systematic theology in a mutually enhancing relationship. Systematic theology can contribute to other forms of theology (biblical, historical, and practical) by providing theological foundations and coherence for advanced work in these disciplines.

SYSTEMATIC THEOLOGY, CHRISTIAN DOCTRINE, AND DIFFERENT INSTITUTIONAL SETTINGS

In spite of ebb and flow in the effectiveness of the partnership between congregational ministries and systematic theology, it must be affirmed that both have made positive contributions to the work of the church. Both can be devotional, pastoral, and confessional. However, the presentation of core Christian beliefs and practices within systematic theology classes at the university or seminary tends to differ from the manner in which they are treated on the congregational level. While statements like "Jesus is Lord" are rightly proclaimed from the pulpit as Christian truths, they may be so carefully examined in a systematic theology class that students unused to this context and method might be at worst offended and at best bored silly. Why do theologians ask questions about things that every Christian knows are true? Do they lack faith, or are they just inveterate navel gazers? Actually, neither is necessarily the case.

Systematic theologians have a different job to do in the academic classroom than preachers do from the pulpit. While some theologians may be ordained, in general they are exercising a different spiritual gift in the class-room and have a different vocation (spiritual calling) than the pastor. While a pastor may have the gift of preaching and/or evangelism, the systematic theologian in a university or seminary classroom probably has the gift of teaching. That teaching gift may be expressed through interactions with students in or out of the classroom, but in some cases is best expressed through theological writing. For theologians such as the medieval scholar Thomas Aquinas, readers are the audience, students, and congregation who benefit most from their teaching gift.

When we realize that theologians and pastors have different spiritual gifts, it may be easier to understand why they do their jobs so differently. Pastors preach, proclaiming God's word. That is a very exciting and impor-tant job. However, theologians also have an important job to do, and it also serves the church. Systematic theologians teach Christians how to under-stand and apply the truths proclaimed from the pulpit, including how those truths fit together in a coherent whole. This job is vital because, as we have seen throughout Christian history, not all Christians agree on these matters. Christians and non-Christians alike sometimes have complex questions about Christianity, and systematic theologians have experience thinking through and answering these questions. By becoming knowledgeable about the Bible, methods of biblical interpretation, church history, Christian doc-trine, and philosophical methods of reasoning and also by becoming expe-rienced applying this knowledge to theological problems, systematic the-ologians are constantly in training to respond to crises of faith and debates within the church.

While systematic theology has undoubtedly been valuable to the church as a whole, there are valid critiques of the discipline that must be considered. As previously mentioned, contemporary churches may (perhaps rightly) challenge systematic theology's neglect of its pastoral roots and ap-plications. However, even this problem may be understood in light of a pro-found shift that occurred in all academic disciplines with the rise of secular humanism two centuries ago. As more and more educated people drifted from the Christian faith and embraced humanistic philosophies, theologians (especially in Europe) found that they had to address a different audience. No longer could they assume that everyone they taught in a classroom or through their writing would be Christian. Some theologians, for example Friedrich Schleiermacher in nineteenth-century Germany, began to address the "cultured despisers" of religion. Their work and spiritual gift was not just teaching, but evangelism. The questions addressed in such theological treatises are not those of the church but of skeptics. The language used in these works is not the devotional language of the faithful but the elevated discourse of the educated elite. Such theology is thus almost unintelligible and certainly comes across as irrelevant in both style and content to most people in the church. Understandably, this kind of theological writing has caused some Christians to reject theology altogether.

When Christians read theology that aims to defend the faith to those who have rejected Christianity (not to assist those who are already faithful to grow in faith), they are likely to encounter questions, ideas, and language that are foreign, irrelevant, or even offensive to them. Christians who are not theologians—rightly perceiving that this work is not for them—may dismiss *all* systematic theology, mistakenly assuming this particular kind of theological writing as representative of the whole. Theological study can help Christians to discern between apologetic theology (intended for non-Christians) and confessional theology (intended for believers). Both are important, but it is necessary to evaluate each on its own terms, considering the intentions and audience in order to understand the content.

There is yet another significant critique that is raised within the discipline itself, namely that the needs met by the work produced in this field are those of an elite minority, while the theological concerns of the world's suffering majority tend to be ignored. The majority of systematic theological work has been and continues to be produced those who are highly educated. Throughout history, access to such education has been more easily available to those of the higher socioeconomic classes, particularly men. Even now, the field of systematic theology is dominated by white Euro-American men with doctoral degrees, though people of all nations, races, economic backgrounds, and genders are influencing the field in ever increasing numbers. It is very important to remember that during the earliest centuries of Christianity, the most significant theological work was produced in Africa. Athanasius of Alexandria in Egypt and Augustine of Hippo in present-day Algeria are just two of the early church leaders who laid the foundations of Christian doctrine in ways still essential to the church and the field of systematic theology.

At this point in history, however, systematic theologians as a group don't accurately and proportionately represent the people they purport to serve—either in the classroom or in the church. As people outside this elite demographic group are joining theological faculties, writing, and teaching in academic settings, they are drawing on their own pastoral and congregational experiences and addressing the concerns of the broader Christian community, reconnecting theology to congregational life in ways that may be more faithful to the origins of Christian theology.

SO WHAT? WHAT SYSTEMATIC
THEOLOGY CAN DO FOR YOU

As a result of the misunderstandings and concerns describe above, many students have low expectations of what they can get from a systematic theology course. They may hope for nothing more from it than to fulfill a degree requirement. However, those who teach systematic theology and write the books students read in these classes hope for more: Studying systematic theology should deepen students' appreciation of the meaning of Christian faith and practice in a lasting way.

What does it mean to think theologically in every aspect of daily life? How can systematic theology help Christians to live out their calling effectively? These may at first seem like strange questions. Every teacher of systematic theology knows that most of her students will not become theologians. Quite frankly, becoming a professional theologian is a perilous path to take. A great deal of formal education is required, all the way through the doctoral degree. At the end of that arduous and expensive process, there is little hope for employment. And if one does manage to find a position in this highly competitive field, it really must be understood as a ministry: Pay is relatively low compared to other professions that require equivalent educational preparation and even compared to other academic fields, while workload is considerable. Teaching must be balanced with scholarly output—presenting public lectures, publishing articles and books, reviewing and editing other theologians' work, among many other tasks. Beyond all this, a theologian must remain connected to the church, for no spiritual gift is employed faithfully unless it builds up the body of Christ. Theologians may provide pulpit supply as guest preachers, contribute to Christian education curricula of various kinds, and even teach or lecture in local congregations. Furthermore, the systematic theologian must do all of this work faithfully in a context where his very vocation is suspect: Many students and fellow church goers assume that their life's work and spiritual calling have nothing meaningful to contribute to the church and perhaps may even be needlessly divisive. This is not an attractive career path. There is no reason to become a theologian unless this is the very purpose to which one is fitted by God, a spiritual vocation.

Since most Christians, then, will not become systematic theologians, there must be something other than professional training to be gained from studying theology. In fact, there are many ways that any student can expect to benefit from studying systematic theology. First, every Christian can benefit from learning how to apply and integrate the resources that theologians use to do their work: scriptures, the Christian tradition, reason, and practical experience. For example, in the New Testament, the apostle Paul frequently reflects on, interprets, and applies Hebrew scriptures, Greek philosophy, and congregational experiences to address matters of Christian faith and practice in a pastoral way. He is not only an apostle but a theologian. Like other theologians throughout history, Paul carefully considers his audience as he makes theological statements, using different language and drawing on different resources when he is addressing fellow Jews than he does when he is addressing Greeks:

> For though I am free with respect to all, I have made myself a slave to all, so that I might win more of them. To the Jews I became as a Jew, in order to win Jews. To those under the law I became as one under the law (though I myself am not under the law) so that I might win those under the law. To those outside the law I became as one outside the law (though I am not free from God's law but am under Christ's law) so that I might win those outside the law. To the weak I became weak, so that I might win the weak. I have become all things to all people, that I might by all means save some. I do it all for the sake of the Gospel, so that I may share in its blessings. (1 Corinthians 9:19–23 NRSV)

Paul wrote this letter to the Christians of Corinth specifically to address theological and practical questions and internal church conflicts as a pastoral leader and theologian. These Christians were not Jewish, but Greek. Some of their problems arose from misunderstandings of the Hebrew scriptures and Jewish theological assumptions about Jesus, the apostles, and Jewish church leaders. Paul's letters labor to explain to them, in terms that they as Greeks could understand, such complex and profound Hebrew theological concepts as spiritual wisdom and resurrection as well as uniquely Christian beliefs, such as the meaning of the crucifixion and Lord's Supper.

As we can see from biblical examples of theology, the method and content of theological reflection learned in a systematic theology course can be applied to resolve confusion about theological questions and to resolve church conflicts. Theological language can even have a liturgical use. In fact, that was the intention of some biblical and early church theological writing. The first verses of John 1, for example, both explain and proclaim the identity of Jesus Christ as the divine being who orders and gives meaning to creation, the word—*logos* in Greek, the same word from which we derive the English word "logic." These verses are written in a liturgical style, in other words to be read aloud in a worship service. They would have been particularly meaningful in the worship life of any early Christian converts more deeply influenced by Greek philosophy than by Judaism.

The early Christian theologians and church leaders who gathered in Nicea to evaluate and respond to the mistaken theological teachings of Arius also composed a statement to be used in worship, the Nicene Creed. This short affirmation of Christian belief in the Father, Son, and Holy Ghost, together with a brief but poetic explanation of the relationship between Son and Father as "light from light, true God from true God," was created for use by local churches. Congregations recited the short creed together as a regular part of worship, affirming their faith while simultaneously resolving a debate over complex theological concepts. By presenting church doctrines in a way that congregations could embrace in weekly worship, the early theologians ensured that their theological work was relevant and accessible to the church. Today, theologians like the Korean Methodist Chung Hyun Kyung sometimes also express their theological reflection in liturgical form for the benefit of the global church at worship.

However, systematic theologians are just as accountable as preachers, evangelists, and prophets to the criteria Jesus gave us for distinguishing between false and faithful teachers:

> Beware of false prophets, who come to you in sheep's clothing but inwardly are ravenous wolves. You will know them by their fruits. Are grapes gathered from thorns, or figs from thistles? In the same way, every good tree bears good fruit, but the bad tree bears bad fruit. A good tree cannot bear bad fruit, nor can a bad tree bear good fruit. Every tree that does not bear good fruit is cut down and thrown into the fire. Thus you will know them by their fruits. Not everyone who says to me, "Lord, Lord" will enter the kingdom of heaven, but only one who does the will of my Father in heaven. (Matthew 7:15–21 NRSV)

As Jesus explained, authentic theological claims will be fruitful not just for understanding but for living. Furthermore, not just the individual, but also the entire community of faith, and even society as a whole should benefit from the spiritual fruits of wisdom, maturity, and compassion that one would expect to be born of a lifetime of continued theological reflection.

One fruit that systematic theology can bear in our work, home and social lives is an increased ability to identify and respond to just and unjust situations. For example, in the 1930s, while Nazism and fascism were on the rise in Europe and Jim Crow laws institutionalized racial oppression in the

United States, American theologian Reinhold Niebuhr published this convicting theological analysis of human nature: He observed that although individuals may develop habits of good moral behavior, when these same individuals participate as members of a larger group, they allow or participate in many of that group's unjust behaviors.

This observation is not just a theological abstraction: Most people have experienced this phenomenon that Niebuhr describes. For example, some of us may have, at least once, stayed silent as a public speaker made a disparaging remark about people who differ from us in gender, physical or mental ability, social class, race, or culture. Others of us may have remained silent rather than volunteering our help while someone in our circle of acquaintance is burdened with excessive or unpleasant tasks. On a larger scale, many of us may have remained passive (possibly out of fear or feelings of powerlessness) as our government pursues foreign or domestic policies we consider to be immoral.

Yet while Niebuhr's assertion about how an individual's moral behavior differs when alone from when part of a group may seem to be supported by personal experience and observation, he did not stop there. He made a further claim that upset the intellectual currents of both his time and ours. Niebuhr argued that human nature is such that improved education, even when it leads to better reasoning, will not correct the inherent injustices of group behavior. Human reason, he argued, is merely the servant of self-interest. Therefore, unlike many theological and political liberals, he believed that not consciousness-raising education but rather force or the threat of force (including the threat of negative economic consequences, organizational censure, and even nonviolent resistance) are necessary to force groups to change unjust laws and practices. Many disagreed with Niebuhr when he first made these claims in his book *Moral Man and Immoral Society* in 1935. By 1945, however, in the aftermath of World War II, Niebuhr's prophetic theological insights grew to have a larger influence.

Later in the century, Niebuhr's theological work influenced Martin Luther King Jr. and the civil rights movement. While doing postgraduate studies, including a Ph.D. in systematic theology at Boston University, King came to agree with Niebuhr that better education would not be sufficient to change white Southern attitudes toward segregation. The civil rights movement ultimately succeeded, at least in part, due to King's embrace of Niebuhr's theological assertion that the power structures of segregation could only be overcome by a nonviolent resistance empowered by black religious beliefs. Though many have emphasized the influence of Gandhi's teachings about nonviolent resistance on King's thought and work, King—

as a theologian, pastor, and civil rights leader—was also strongly influenced by the Bible, particularly Jeremiah's prophetic call to a nation that was in decline and heading for disaster and Jesus' teachings on peace and suffering. Thus, not only King's black Baptist church upbringing and ministry but also his extensive theological study of the prophets in Hebrew scripture and Reinhold Niebuhr's writings on human nature significantly shaped him as a leader of the civil rights movement.

Though most of us will not do anything as dramatic as leading a civil rights movement, it is almost certain that we will encounter injustice or at least apathy toward justice issues in groups to which we belong. If we are regularly studying theological works such as those of Niebuhr, King, and others such as John Wesley, then we, like King, may find ourselves better equipped with the courage to say and do the things that will move our groups toward justice and Christ-like love.

As illustrated by King's example, learning and practicing the systematic theological method (understanding the historical tradition of the faith, philosophical reasoning, and lived experience in light of Christian scriptures) can help us to discern God's calling on our lives and to live it out faithfully. Practiced rightly, theology should further the kingdom of God by inviting each of us to deeper understanding of scriptures, of the historical faith community, and even of our own experience—particularly the connections between all of these. This improved understanding is not just an opportunity to gain knowledge for its own sake but should be translated into a more mature way of living out God's call on our lives as Christian men and women.

9

YOUTH MINISTRY: TAKING A SEAT
AT THE GROWN-UPS' TABLE

Kara Powell and Steve Gerali

*F*reezing temperatures, shoveling sidewalks, living off of canned soup for days. Being snowed in was something Doug hardly ever enjoyed.

But this December the snow felt more like a gift than a curse.

Although Doug's son, Micah, had been home from college for a week, Doug had hardly seen him. When Doug left for work in the morning, Micah was still fast asleep, trying to erase his sleep deficit from finals week. By the time Doug arrived home, Micah was out to dinner or a movie with friends. As Doug sipped his morning coffee, he wondered if the snow that blanketed the streets and made driving to work impossible would drive him and his son closer together.

Micah stumbled down the stairs and into the kitchen. "Hey dad, is there any more coffee?"

Now there's a new development. When did Micah start drinking coffee? "Sure, I'll make you some."

As Doug went to grind some beans, he realized that the ten minutes it took to make and start drinking a pot of coffee would finally give him a chance to catch up with his son. "So how are your classes going?"

"Pretty well, I guess. Physics was a drag, but the rest were okay. It sure is different than high school."

Doug thought to himself, A lot more expensive, too. Aloud he asked, "What's different about it?"

"There's way more homework, and I feel like all I do is read. The library has become my second home."

Doug poured the coffee grounds into his coffee machine and turned on the machine. Looking out his window, Doug saw the snow was falling even harder. "How was your political science final?"

"It went okay. The reading in that class was the worst. In fact, I don't think I'm going to major in poli sci anymore."

Doug snapped his head and turned toward his son. "You're not? You've wanted to go into politics since you were fifteen years old. You loved student government when you were in high school."

"Yeah, but that was the make-believe world of high school. Studying about it in college is boring."

Doug tried to keep his voice calm as he asked a question he knew could easily turn into a fight. "What about the summer internship you applied for at Congressman Hawley's office?"

"Well, actually, I've got an even better option. I'm applying to be a camp counselor at the Mount Brightley Conference Center."

Doug could feel his pulse rising. "You're giving up a political internship to spend a summer at camp?"

Micah shrugged. "Well, I'm thinking about majoring in youth ministry, and if I spend a summer at camp, I can get college credit for it."

Thoughts raced through Doug's mind. Youth ministry? You're opting away from politics to hang out with a bunch of fourteen year olds? You'd rather be a glorified babysitter than impact the nation's public policy?

Micah had so much potential. High school valedictorian, senior class president, captain of the debate club. Why would Micah waste all that to become a youth pastor? He could only hope that Micah would change his mind by spring break.

Whether you're a parent like Doug, a student like Micah, or simply someone who cares enough about the congregation and the academy to read this book, you've probably noticed some of the attitudes toward youth ministry described in the above story. In some cases, youth ministry is viewed positively because parents have fond memories of the guidance their own teenage children received from youth workers. Like the other religion and philosophy disciplines, however, youth ministry is often a victim of the divide between the church and the college, although it suffers in a different way. While the disciplines of biblical studies, philosophy, and theology are sometimes viewed as cold and irrelevant, the discipline of youth ministry is sometimes viewed as fluffy child's play. Other courses of study may be feared because of the perception that they turn students into atheists or make them too liberal or too conservative, but they're viewed as academic heavyweights. Unfortunately, youth ministry can be perceived as glorified babysitting and as such does not require academic investment.

Together, we have more than forty years of experience in professional youth ministry and more than fifteen years of teaching youth ministry in universities and seminaries. Our youth ministry courses are as challenging as any at our university. Like every other youth ministry professor we know, we take it as a compliment when students moan and groan about the work-load in our courses. The point isn't that the classes are difficult but that students are required to learn critical thinking skills and apply them to complex ministry situations. Developing the skills to effectively minister and mentor adolescents and their families is hard work and time intensive, and the complexity of youth ministry requires extensive training. The discipline of youth ministry is characterized by four realities that need to be defined, described, and applied to both the church and the academy.

REALITY 1: YOUTH MINISTRY IS A "REAL JOB"

It was a long way from financial independence, but Doug figured that they were at least making baby steps in the right direction. Before Micah left for college, Doug and Micah had agreed that if Micah paid for gas and insurance, he could take his dad's old sedan to school. Given that his sedan was a few thousand miles shy of the nearest junkyard, Doug had volunteered to pay for all maintenance and repairs. Today that meant two new tires.

Doug had avoided bringing up Micah's major for the first half of spring break, but he couldn't skirt it any longer. He had to find out what Micah had decided.

Doug put his coffee cup down on the wooden table in the car mechanic's waiting room. "So Micah, how's your youth ministry class coming?"

Micah looked up from the car magazine he had been skimming. "It's great. It's the first class I've had that relates to real life."

"So are you still planning on majoring in youth ministry?"

Micah sipped his coffee. "You bet. I really think it's what God wants me to do."

That's funny, Doug thought. . . . I thought God wanted me to work hard and save money in a college fund for you for the last twelve years, and now you're spending it on something I'm not that excited about. If you wanted to be a senior pastor, at least that would be a real profession. Youth ministry doesn't seem like much of a job.

Unfortunately, leaders and members of both the church and the academy often share Doug's belief that youth ministry is a precursor to "real pastoring" or a "real job." While some do receive initial training and experience in youth ministry and then shift to other ministries, two bodies of evidence give credence to youth ministry as a valid profession. The first is the history of the evolution of youth ministry. While an extensive treatment of the history of youth ministry lies beyond the scope of this chapter, a brief summary of its development helps explain why youth workers need to be viewed as professionals.

Mark Cannister in *Starting Right: Thinking Theologically about Youth Ministry* (edited by Chap Clark, Kenda Creasy Dean, and Dave Rahn) explains that the roots of youth ministry lie deep in the history of Christian education. Efforts to educate new converts through both informal and formal religious instruction were neglected during the Renaissance era. Christian scholars usually chose to participate in secular disciplines rather than in religious education. During the sixteenth century Protestant Reformation, there was a resurgence of interest in Christian education as Martin Luther argued for the education of all people and John Calvin emphasized the educational responsibility of the church in lifestyle transformation. Two centuries later, Sunday school classes focusing on both spiritual nurture and basic literacy education multiplied in England and the United States.

As both the Sunday school movement and the work of the Young Men's Christian Association (YMCA) resulted in thousands of conversions, many pastors and leaders focused their efforts on stimulating parallel revival movements. One revivalist pastor, Horace Bushnell of Connecticut, decided to focus his energy on nurturing existing Christians, a move that soon became characteristic of Christian education. The work of the Society for Christian Endeavor in the late 1800s reflects this Bushnellian emphasis on the church's nurture of its own children and young people. By the turn of the century, nearly all major denominations had formed youth societies modeled after Christian Endeavor. They emphasized spiritual awakening among young people who were already seeking after God and were generally also already attending church.

As the developmental stage of adolescence became recognized as a legitimate sociological phenomenon in the 1930s and 1940s, so did the concept of a missional ministry to that age group. In the 1940s, Jim Rayburn started the Young Life Campaign in the United States, and Billy Graham preached at the first Youth for Christ rally. Unlike Christian Endeavor and the youth societies that focused on nurturing the young people of the church, these newer ministries focused on winning converts. As Christian Endeavor had done in the late 1800s, the success of these parachurch movements caught the attention of denominational leaders. Christian education for youth again became associated not just with the nurture of those already inside the church walls, but also with outreach to those outside.

For the last several decades, church and parachurch youth organizations have recruited and hired professional youth ministers to both evangelize and nurture adolescents. Churches with sufficient resources realize that the one hour Sunday school model of the 1800s is inadequate to address the complexities of youth culture. They seek well-trained part-time and full-time professionals who can educate and disciple the youth of the church while simultaneously leading innovative and creative outreach into the community and its school campuses. While the first recorded full-time youth minister in America was hired in St. Louis in 1937, by the 1970s "youth pastor" was an established position on evangelical churches' pastoral staffs. From the 1960s to 1990s, youth ministry as a profession exploded, and colleges and seminaries responded by offering courses in the subject.

As youth ministry has evolved historically into a valued profession, it has become more than a stepping-stone on the path to a senior pastorate. The second body of evidence that points to youth ministry's professional status is the empirical research on the age and stage of youth practitioners. Several years ago when Azusa Pacific University considered launching a major in youth ministry, some wondered whether we were doing a disservice to students who might not make youth ministry their permanent vocation. While there is no empirical research examining the job placement potential or youth ministry longevity of students who major in youth ministry, our decision to birth a youth ministry major was partly informed by a recent vast cross-denominational survey of twenty-four hundred full-time youth ministry practitioners. As Merton Strommen, Karen E. Jones, and Dave Rahn of Link Institute observe in *Youth Ministry That Transforms*, there is a current "graying" of youth ministers. In their survey, the dominant age cluster of practicing youth workers was thirty to thirty-nine year olds, comprising 41.5 percent of those surveyed. Second was forty to forty-nine year olds at 23.2 percent. Only 28.8 percent of professional youth workers were twenty-nine years old and younger. A parallel finding is the length of youth ministry tenure. Over 47 percent of those surveyed had been in youth ministry ten years or longer. Only 14.9 percent answered that they had been in youth ministry three years or less.

It seems likely that this trend of staying in the field of youth ministry for more than a decade is only going to intensify. As a profession, youth ministry has reached critical mass. The needs of the church and the response of the academy are together creating new momentum and synergy. Due to the growing number of youth workers, more academic and professional training is available. This training, in turn, entices more into the field, which leads to the need for further training.

REALITY 2: YOUTH MINISTRY IS MULTIFACETED

While youth ministry is a practical field of study, its practicality is grounded in solid, academic study. Students of youth ministry must master an understanding of developmental theories from the social sciences, cultural theories from societal studies, models and theories for interpreting scripture from biblical studies and theology, and pedagogical approaches from education. Often youth ministry lacks effectiveness because uneducated youth workers attempt to reproduce models of ministry without understanding the theories behind them. Theory and practice work in tandem in youth ministry. While the pragmatic side of youth ministry is the visible, tangible part of ministry, its academic depth gives youth ministry its multifaceted dynamic. When it comes to academic theory, effective youth workers should become and remain constant students of God's word and theology, culture, and adolescence.

Youth Ministers Are Constant Students of God's Word and Theology

Being a student of God's word requires discipline. The apostle Paul challenged Timothy to study God's word to handle it effectively and show himself a workman approved by God (2 Timothy 2:15). Paul's challenge is not just to be a reader of God's word but to be a student of it.

Our students often ask us, "Do you really need to get a degree in Bible to be a student of the Bible? Isn't the Holy Spirit the one who 'leads us in all truth'?" While we understand that the Holy Spirit teaches the believer, we realize that God has established patterns throughout scripture and history that need to be observed. In the Old Testament era, God established a school of prophets under great leaders like Samuel and Elijah. In the New Testament time period, the church and its leadership became subject to the teaching of the apostles and others. Throughout history the seats of higher education were originally established as centers of religious education. Many universities started as schools of theology or seminaries and over time began to develop knowledge in other disciplines. This came about as the result of an integrated approach to theology in the secular disciplines. The university became a center where theology could be explored in relation to math, art, science, and language. Over time a shift occurred, and God became absent in the modern university. The fields of youth ministry and practical theology have attempted to regain this ground by reintegrating theology and other disciplines as they relate to the rapidly and continuously changing adolescent population.

Being a student of scripture doesn't just mean finding an application for a particular text. It also involves understanding a proper interpretation of the text. Unless youth workers have proper hermeneutical approaches to understanding scripture, they might fall into the common dangerous errors of proof texting and/or universalizing principles. For example, at one point in youth ministry it was considered sin to attend movies, go to bowling alleys, dance, and play card games. Members of the evangelical church believed that these things were associated with the world and supported their views with scriptural texts regarding "separation from the world" and "avoiding any appearance of evil." Proper hermeneutics understands contexts, interpretation, grammatical composition, syntax, genre, and contextualization. Youth workers need to learn a proper method of scriptural *exegesis* rather than *eisegesis*. Stone and Duke, in *How to Think Theologically*, define exegesis as the "analysis and explanation of the meaning of scripture drawn from close, careful attention to the language of the text" and eisegesis as the "practice of imposing one's own ideas on scripture rather than drawing out the meaning."

If youth workers are called to be constant students of God's word, they must also become scholars of theology. Simply put, theology is the study of Christian doctrines as they inform us about who God is and what he does juxtaposed against who we are and what we do. Theology answers fundamental questions about life purpose, afterlife, relationship with God, morality, ethics, and identity. It shapes and informs an individual's worldview or perspective on life. Adolescents are coming into a life stage where they are beginning to wrestle with these complex issues. Only youth workers who are theologically equipped can meet adolescents in that process.

Youth workers are also students of practical theology. Practical theology involves the integration of theology into personal and church disciplines like worship, counseling and care, communication, learning, and decision making. As a practical theologian, a youth worker serves students as mentors, teachers, guides, counselors, and shepherds. Effective youth ministry is measured by legacy. Success of the youth worker as a practical theologian comes when adolescents become adult followers of Christ, integrate themselves into the church, and are committed to a life of obedient and joyful service.

Being a student of God's word and theology makes a youth worker a prime candidate for ministry in a variety of contexts. Church youth ministry roles can include youth pastors, pastoral counselors, youth worship directors, and life coaches. It also opens doors in parachurch ministries (e.g., Youth For Christ, Young Life, Fellowship of Christian Athletes, Campus

Crusade), as campus pastors in private schools and colleges, campus ministry directors and staff at secular universities, and Bible teachers and coaches in Christian schools.

Youth Ministers Are Constant Students of an Ever-Changing Culture

The term "cultural relevance" is thrown around regularly in ministry. Many youth workers think that they understand the needs, values, and constructs of a culture if they are in tune to the popular aspects of the culture (i.e., music, media, language). In fact, they may be just borrowing the sights and sounds of the day without being truly relevant. Anyone can tune into popular televison, pick up a few teen magazines, immerse themselves in the top ten tunes, and come away looking like they understand the culture. This does not make them culturally relevant; it just makes them mimics of media.

As students of culture, effective youth workers acquire the skills to be *ethnographers*—people who observe, study, dissect, define, and describe the values, biases, norms, needs, beliefs, traditions, ideals, attitudes, roles, ethnicity, language, art, and communication of a cultural community within a broader community. This also involves an understanding of the historical context that a group and/or community owns, allowing ethnographers to track similarities and differences from generation to generation.

Youth workers who become constant students of culture can work with kids in a broader context and remain culturally relevant for life. Relevance is only effective when the youth worker also becomes an *ethnologist*. While *ethnography* is the study of a culture, *ethnology* is the comparative study of two or more cultures. Culturally relevant youth workers are constantly comparing the culture of present adolescents against their own cultural imprint. This can create cognitive dissonance requiring the uncomfortable experience of change, or *contextualization*.

Contextualization forces youth workers to evaluate, re-evaluate and redefine their own frames of reference. This is at the heart of *incarnational* youth ministry. At incarnation, Jesus "became flesh and dwelt among us" (John 1:14). It is important to note that while God becomes human, we are already human. Thus, incarnational ministry loses something in the translation. However, effective youth ministry models this principle when youth workers change their frame of reference to "become like" (understand and relate to) teenagers without compromising, yet challenging their Christian convictions. It also means that youth workers become visible, tangible representatives of an invisible Christ. The apostle Paul also develops this concept in 1 Corinthians 9:22 when he speaks of becoming "all things to all men" in order to reach them.

This facet of youth ministry broadens the scope of opportunity for a professional youth worker. Mission boards increasingly call youth pastors to cross-cultural and urban ministries. According to the United Nations Population Fund (formerly called the United Nations Fund for Population Activities: UNFPA), more than half of the world's population is under the age of twenty-five, with over 40 percent of the population in fifty-seven developing countries being under the age of fifteen. This has generated the need for youth ministry experts in modern missions. Many of our students are challenged to consider youth ministry in a global context rather than a suburban, middle-class, Western context.

Youth Ministers Are Constant Students of Adolescence

Teenagers are in a unique life stage known as adolescence. This developmental stage has been studied intensely over the last century. Earlier we talked about the twentieth-century movement to reach adolescents for Christ. This movement was fueled by a parallel movement in the social science community to understand this phenomenon of adolescence. Notions of a transition from childhood to adulthood date back to Plato, Socrates, and Aristotle, but these views were never fully developed. From the Middle Ages to the Age of Enlightenment, children were viewed as miniature adults. G. Stanley Hall, the father of the scientific study of adolescence, developed a historical perspective of these transitional notions from literature and biography. In his two-volume work entitled *Adolescence*, Hall cites the impact of the medieval church on the hearts and minds of youth as the impetus for these adolescents taking vows of chastity, service, and entrance into lives of sanctity. Theologians at the turn of the last century also began to recognize the distinction of adolescence. As early as 1877, Keim in his work entitled *The History of Jesus of Nazareth* (volume III) identifies Jesus as choosing adolescents as disciples. Keim states:

> An age of not much more than twenty years is plainly indicated in the case of the four first called, notably of the sons of Zebedee, and also of James the younger, of the youth in Judea and Gethsemane, nay, indeed, of most of them, for they are represented as coming directly from the houses of their parents, and Jesus cautions them against preferring their parents to their Teacher, against jealous fancies and ebullitions of temper, and administers to them truly paternal censures. (279)

Keim goes on to state that idealism, characteristic of adolescent development, spared them from the "pharisaic bondage" that their elders had internalized. Adolescence made these individuals prime candidates to become disciples. Keim's focus on the disciples' youthfulness reflects the ground swell of the concept of adolescence and developmental theory that peaked at the end of the nineteenth and beginning of the twentieth centuries.

The formation of the first public high school in America in 1875 and compulsory legislation designed to protect minors from exploitation in the labor force put adolescence in the limelight of industrialized culture. Many psychologists, sociologists, and anthropologists formed theories about the individual's passage from childhood into adulthood. These theories of development began to cut across and influence many disciplines. Professionals with expertise in the area of adolescent development began to emerge in the arenas of business and marketing, medicine, education, mental health professions, social work, and religion. Subsequently the formation of developmental theories influenced the patterns and formation of youth ministry.

A developmental approach to youth ministry is a multidisciplinary perspective that hinges on two basic foundational concerns: (1) helping adolescents successfully navigate developmental tasks, which requires age-appropriate ministries, and (2) holistic balance or ministry to the whole person. These foundational concerns are played out as two intersecting axioms in shaping how ministry is done to adolescents.

The *person* of an adolescent is comprised of five specific dimensions: physiological or biological, intellectual or cognitive, affective or emotive, sociological or interpersonal, and moral or spiritual. These dimensions develop at a rapid rate through adolescence. An adolescent must work through the difficulties that arise out of the growth process in each dimension in order to become a physically mature, sound thinking, relationally equipped, emotionally stable, God-honoring, autonomous adult. A developmental structure to youth ministry seeks to produce such adults.

As professionals with expertise in human growth and development, youth workers understand the cognitive shifts in adolescence and accommodate educational and communication styles to connect with that age group. The youth worker understands the physiological and sexual maturation processes and their effects on an adolescent's drives, desires, and emotions. The sociological or interpersonal dimension shapes the adolescent's identity and intimacy skills. The spiritual dimension is where faith formation, moral development, and value clarification and internalization take place. An effective youth worker also ministers to families by assisting parents or training parental surrogates to meet the holistic developmental needs of an adolescent.

As a student of adolescence, the professional youth worker can minister to adolescents in nontraditional youth ministry settings. These settings range from residential centers for foster care, to drug and substance treatment agencies, to crisis pregnancy centers. Some youth workers have utilized their training as experts in the area of adolescence and stepped in as advocates with the juvenile court system and police departments. Others have used their expertise in physiology to start sports ministries, coach school sports, or work with municipal park and recreation districts. Many of these youth workers use their undergraduate youth ministry education as a foundation for later graduate work in counseling, social work, or pastoral care.

Youth ministry is multifaceted. An effective twenty-first century professional youth worker is well defined as a theologian, philosopher, counselor, developmental psychologist, ethnographer, educator, pastor, missionary, parent, coach, ethnologist, advocate, and mentor.

REALITY 3: YOUTH MINISTRY IS REFLECTIVE

To use common vernacular, youth ministry has been labeled more about the "heart" than the "head." This label reflects the belief that youth ministry is not a discipline that requires much serious reflection. All a youth worker allegedly needs to do is hang out with kids.

While relational, incarnational ministry and experiential worship are two important components of an effective youth ministry, they need to be undergirded by an ongoing commitment to solid theological reflection. Following the "DECIDE" practical theology paradigm presented in chapter 11, we have found that our students benefit from an integration of the Wesleyan Quadrilateral. In the third step, as students and youth workers examine the central resources of faith to assess current issues and practices, the Wesleyan Quadrilateral is helpful in its description of four sources of authority: scripture, tradition, reason, and experience. By scripture, we mean the sixty-six books of the Old and New Testaments. Tradition refers to the practices and beliefs of the church throughout history. Reason includes both common sense and logic, while experience is the inner witness of the Holy Spirit both individually and corporately.

Part of our job as youth ministry professors is to help students learn how to use these four resources as part of the thorough reflection that leads to more effective ministry. Recently, a local youth pastor guest lectured in one of our youth ministry classes. His ministry is committed to loving, serving, and mentoring at-risk students in Pasadena, California. While his ministry philosophy has scripture as its ultimate foundation, he has also integrated reason into his methodology. His ministry has been heavily influenced by the work of the well-respected Search Institute, which has identified forty developmental assets that teens need in order to thrive. These assets are grouped into categories such as support, boundaries, commitment to learning, positive values, social competencies, and positive identity. The more assets students possess, the more likely they are to thrive. This youth pastor has integrated this valuable social science research into his mentoring program. Instead of merely asking his volunteer mentors to play some sort of vague empowering and encouraging role in troubled kids' lives, he gives them each a list of the forty developmental assets. A major component of their role as mentors is to identify which resources their kids lack and then to find creative ways to provide their kids with those resources.

That is just one of an almost infinite list of examples of solid youth ministry reflection that embraces both heart and head. The most effective youth workers realize that basing their ministry practices only on anecdotal evidence or on what's worked in the past might yield some fruit, but it will fall short of the full harvest that comes from ongoing practical theology reflection.

REALITY 4: YOUTH MINISTRY IS ENTREPRENEURIAL

Youth ministry is a relatively new profession. The church and Christian community ask youth workers to reach and minister effectively to an ever growing at-risk population. The scope of youth ministry is also broadening to encompass many different venues and expand globally. Youth ministry has integrated multiple disciplines, making it multifaceted. All of this suggests that youth ministry is entrepreneurial.

Usually the word "entrepreneurial" conjures up negative pictures of powerful, capitalistic, cutthroat, empire-building, lone-ranger leaders. We realize that the church is not a corporation, and ministry is not a commodity to be marketed. When we describe youth ministry as entrepreneurial, we mean that the field's future is wide open, the sky is the limit, and the horizon is bright. An entrepreneurial perspective includes four elements: vision, innovation, change, and risk.

The vision of youth ministry is expanding. Where we once saw youth ministry limited to a more affluent Western culture, the vision has expanded to include adolescents worldwide. The process of extending youth ministry's view to a global perspective is still in its infant stages, and much still remains to be done. Youth workers must expose their churches to the growing needs of kids by doing ministry across cultural boundaries and taking kids to minister in other cultures. As youth ministry professors, we are instilling a vision in our students to care for the plight of children and teenagers all over the world. Youth ministry is beginning to address issues like a growing HIV/AIDS epidemic that is killing teenagers in Africa or leaving them homeless, alone, and lost. It is bringing hope to teens in eastern Europe and contesting the cancer of apathy in North American and western European teens.

While this groundswell is just beginning, much more can and should be done. Youth ministry must create a movement of concern and action for the homelessness of countless teens in war-torn countries throughout the Middle East and Africa. It must become an active voice and powerful force to combat the problem of sexual slavery of teenagers in some Asian cultures. It should deliberately mobilize the church to arrest the increasing rate of teenage street kids turning to prostitution and drug addiction in South America. Youth ministry has an obligation to bring healing to a world of hurting adolescents. A frontier still largely untouched is the opportunity to connect with countless adolescents worldwide through cyberspace. When youth ministry sees a world that is largely comprised of unreached adolescents, it should also see a world of opportunity.

Entrepreneurial youth ministry thrives on innovation. It is a field that requires flexibility and creativity. This type of innovation breeds an environment where creative teams can flourish. One area of emerging creativity in youth ministry is technology. The Internet is redefining the way teens view relationships. Youth ministry must be innovative in order to minister effectively to this shifting understanding of relationships. A few years ago we became aware of this relational shift when one of our students described his most meaningful relationship. He told us that he met regularly with his youth pastor who mentored him. While this does not sound unusual, it soon became evident to us that he had never seen this man face to face. He had met this youth pastor online and for a couple years met regularly with him in cyberspace. Relationship was immediately redefined for us. The innovation of youth ministry is to take these data and creatively attempt to answer the question of how "relationship with Christ" will look to this teenager.

Constant change also marks an entrepreneurial environment. Youth ministry is marked by constant change, so students of the discipline must learn to embrace it or consider another area of ministry. Youth ministers need to thrive a bit on chaos. The practices that worked in ministry last year won't work this year. The cultural landscape is constantly shifting and nudging ministry to change, sometimes by default. Youth workers cannot be threatened by change, nor can they hold on too tightly to programs and ideas. Youth ministry becomes entrepreneurial when change is accepted as the norm.

Finally, youth ministry is entrepreneurial when it takes risks. Youth workers need to think outside the box. The problem with this is that very often the church may not be on the same page. Taking risks often means abandoning some things that are viewed as sacred. Thinking outside of the box gently pushes the church to get out of its comfort zone and address critical questions regarding why and how we do things the way we do. Risk makes a ministry entrepreneurial, but it must also calculate the cost. Risk without wisdom is reckless. Nevertheless risk is essential to entrepreneurial youth ministry.

CONCLUDING APPLICATION

Doug learned to capitalize on Micah's newly acquired taste for coffee by doing frequent Starbucks runs with his son whenever he came home. They continued to talk about Micah's passion for youth ministry and his coursework. Micah was now in his junior year, and he was more convinced of his calling to youth ministry. One evening Doug decided to call Micah to see how things were going.

"Dad, my internship is really stretching me," Micah said. "I love working with Jason, the youth pastor at First Church. He's been doing youth ministry for over fifteen years and really knows his stuff." Micah rambled on, "The past couple weeks have been very hectic. Three students from the local high school were killed in an automobile accident. One of the students was in our youth group."

"Boy, that's terrible. How are you handling that?"

"Well, I'm okay. It was difficult, but it was also very rewarding. Jason really involved me in the entire process. I went with him to minister to the family. I was so glad that I had that counseling course. It was also cool to meet with my youth ministry professors and bounce things off them too. Not only did we meet with the family, but the principal of the high school asked Jason to come to the school and help debrief students. Jason asked me to come along with him. We also planned a special meeting time at the church for students to come for more help. It's been cool to see kids come to know Christ because of this."

"Wow, I didn't think that youth pastors could do stuff like that in the public school."

"Well, we can't talk about Christ unless a kid initiates the conversation, but we can help in a time of crisis if the school invites us. Jason has built great relationships with the administrators of the school. He is really recognized and viewed by the teachers as a colleague in the field of adolescence."

"I guess I'm starting to see youth ministry differently. I didn't realize that youth ministry really could be that diverse and professional. I'm also glad that you are in such a great internship."

"I'm glad too, dad, but that's unusual. Not all of my friends have an internship of the same quality as mine."

While Doug became more enlightened about youth ministry as a profession, Micah verbalized some of the issues that still need to be addressed. Micah is supported and equipped by both the church and the academy. This is unusual, because there still does not exist a consistent synergy between the church and the academy in youth ministry. The church needs well-trained youth workers and could offer resources and support to students in the academy who need venues to connect their theory with practice. Some tangibles could include paid internships, real mentoring (versus loose or nonexistent supervision), and true evaluation (really talking about their strengths, weaknesses, and growth areas).

The academy needs to remain aware of the ever-changing needs of the church. Professors must stay innovative in assessing and meeting the needs of youth workers and adolescents. Many professors in youth ministry are also practitioners, working hands-on with youth workers and adolescents. Along with the church, the academy needs to also take more responsibility to be the gatekeeper of those who think that they are called to youth ministry. Unfortunately, many people want to go into youth ministry for the wrong reasons.

It is our belief that the academy exists to serve the church. The academy becomes the critical training center and breeding ground for innovative thought in youth ministry. Internships, practicum, and hands-on projects become the litmus tests for the youth worker, confirming ministry calling and giftedness. The ongoing synergy between the church and the academy must be an ongoing concern and focal point if youth ministry is to remain effective.

10

PASTORAL MINISTRY: A PARTNERSHIP BETWEEN ACADEMY AND CONGREGATION

Dick Pritchard

The person called by God into full-time pastoral ministry will experience a wonderfully fulfilling and very challenging life. A pastor shares the greatest joys and the deepest sorrows in the lives of others, which creates an awareness of great privilege and great responsibility. Often, the person preparing for pastoral ministry is passionate about the possibilities, somewhat idealistic about the opportunities, and eager to start serving as quickly as possible. Whenever a pastor steps into a new ministry role, there is healthy anticipation about what God will do in this new relationship of pastor and congregation. The difficulty is that the expectations are often different for pastor than for the congregation. This new relationship is like a marriage where expectations are tempered by the realities of sharing life together.

The pastor often sees what is not and what could be, both of which imply needed change. People in congregations tend to use the same language of expectation, but often that means something different to each congregant. Many will want to minimize change. At the beginning of a new pastor transition, my congregation was asked, "What is your vision for our church in the coming years?" The hundreds of responses were posted for all to see. Very few reflected a corporate vision for the church. Virtually all could be labeled "personal agendas," best illustrated by the fact that several were in direct opposition to visions others had named. When a pastor steps into this kind of setting, many factors shape the expectations of the congregation—culture, age, education, denominational tradition, special needs, and more. The pastor has varying degrees of authority to lead, depending on the church tradition and practices. Regardless of the strength of the mandate to lead, the pastor will need to address the multitude of expectations with great discernment and care.

Because of the inherent tension in pastoral leadership, it is vital that the academy and the congregation come to an understanding about the nature of pastoral ministry. Perhaps more than ever before, significant preparation for ministry in response to God's call is absolutely necessary, and the academy is an important partner for this preparation. In addition to more traditional studies, the academy includes experiential opportunities for pastoral candidates that allows classroom learning to be applied and tested. However, it is impossible for every conceivable ministry need to be addressed in the classroom or by experience while in the academy. What then can the academy provide for preparation?

Academic preparation for ministry will be addressed in greater depth below. However, given the limitation of time in the academy and the diversity of expectations and needs alive in the church and the world, it must be admitted up front that educational institutions can only prepare the groundwork for future pastoral ministry. The person preparing for such ministry brings all the influences, good and bad, that have shaped one's life before the academy. One goal of academic preparation is to utilize, refine, reform, and sometimes abandon habits, thoughts, and behavioral patterns. This is done by raising awareness of these patterns and how they can contribute to effectiveness or create potential stress points later in ministry. Students preparing for ministry seldom know the questions that need to be asked or why certain issues are important to understand. A former student, now a full-time pastor of student ministries, recently said that he had been selective in his learning process, retaining only things he deemed important. In pastoral ministry he returned to notes and texts, realizing that the academic requirements had more value than he had realized. If the academy and congregation partner in this process, pastors will benefit from the value of this early preparation and will often seek further development in an academic setting after they have assumed pastoral positions.

TRANSFORMATION AS THE SOURCE OF MINISTRY

All ministry flows out of Christian spirituality. Therefore, to understand how ministry fits into the bigger picture of our relationship with Christ, we will start with a model for spiritual transformation. Envision four concentric circles radiating from a center. The center circle represents a narrative that shapes an individual life and answers the question, "What is your core story?" Core stories represent the primary motivating attitudes in a person's life, whether or not the person is conscious of them. Some of these stories have names like "consumerism," "individualism," "hedonism," and "nationalism." The possibilities are extensive. Christianity's core story can be viewed as participation in a recurring three-part drama. First, humanity experiences brokenness, alienation, and sin. The second scene is found in the Incarnation, when Jesus came into our world and history to bring redemption. The third part of this drama is the experience of progressive transformation as we enter into the redemption that Jesus brought into the world. The drama recurs as growth and ongoing transformation open up new awareness aspects of life that need redemption. One of the academy's primary tasks is to provide the tools for students to identify their operative stories, to discover the implications of those stories, and to consider how those stories can be shaped, redeemed, and transformed by the Gospel.

The next larger circle around the core is labeled "convictions," with the accompanying question, "What do you believe is absolutely true and right?" Every story has inherent convictions that are determined directly by the core story. For example, the core story of consumerism results in the conviction that it is important to buy, to own, and to consume continually. Convictions then determine values, which would be the third and next larger circle. The question here is, "How do invest yourself and your resources?" To follow the example, consumerism gives priority to accumulating material things, although things like relationships and experiences can also be collected and consumed.

The fourth circle is the area of identity and behavior, where one asks the questions, "Who am I, and how do I act in the world?" This is the external part of life that reveals how one sees self, is seen by others, or attempts to be seen by others. It is the above-surface reflection of the inward story, convictions, and values. People often attempt to change this aspect of life while resisting change in the inner circles. A focus on extreme makeovers and the proliferation of self-help publications, secular and Christian, may be examples of this approach.

What does this mean for ministry? The Gospel story of the Fall, Incarnation, and redemption ought to be the core narrative for the Christ follower. Conversion and ongoing transformation are the process of subordinating all other stories to the Gospel. The process of conversion (what Christians often refer to as being born again) involves shifting our allegiance from some other story to following Christ. As we attempt to follow Christ, we discover that he identifies himself as a servant (the source of our word for minister). Internalizing the Gospel story means that Christ's followers become servants and ministers.

Transformation (also referred to as sanctification) occurs as the Gospel story begins to radiate outward and bring about a change in our convictions, values, identity, and behavior. As we move from the inner circle of the story, which all Christians share in common, to the external circle of our public behaviors, we move toward our own specific vocation or calling. In other words, we move from the general model of Jesus as servant to the unique ways in which this servant calling is displayed in our own life. All believers minister, whether they are software engineers, doctors, coaches, or pastors. In each case, our concrete vocation creates times, places, and relationships where God's spirit ministers through us.

PASTORAL MINISTRY

While all Christians are ministers, pastoral ministry has distinguishing characteristics that set it apart from the general practice of ministry (often referred to as lay ministry). The primary task of the pastor is to shepherd (a traditionally dominant biblical image for pastoral ministry) the people of God. As shepherd, a pastor cares for those who follow Christ, calling them to be transformed in their convictions, values, identity, and behavior through the Gospel. The primary means by which pastors shepherd the laity are proclaiming the word of God, engaging believers in the sacraments, and preparing spiritually gifted believers for ministry.

An individual within a congregation can experience God's call to pastoral ministry in many ways. It can happen in adolescence or much later in life. This calling may arise at a significant moment or through a growing awareness. The call may emerge from an inner passion, the influence of those in the community, or both. At times the directive is absolutely clear and unavoidable; at other times it may evolve in exploratory ways. Many individuals are called to full-time pastoral ministry in a role other than senior pastor. Whatever the nature of the call, in most traditions a person responds by beginning a process that ultimately leads to ordination (or some comparable affirmation)—the confirmation of the calling by the pastor, congregation, and those in authority that qualifies one for pastoral ministry.

While the process that leads to ordination begins and ends in the congregational life, the academy is a partner in preparation. Two main reasons exist for this partnership. First, congregations recognize that those called to proclaim God's word, administer the sacraments, and equip the laity need training for these very important tasks. Second, our contemporary culture often expects far more than these basic abilities from pastors. The congregation generally relies on educational institutions to provide this specialized preparation.

THE PERSON CALLED TO MINISTRY

We have stressed that all Christians are called to be ministers because both congregants and pastors tend to have unrealistic expectations of pastors. There is one obvious historical reason for this. The trajectory since biblical times shows an increasing chasm between the pastor and the laity. Over time, this separation led to a passive spectator role for all but pastors. The Reformation's focus on the priesthood of all believers did little to alter this trend. Perhaps more than ever, the pastor is expected by many to be the paid ministry professional. As a result, laypeople often view themselves as the recipients of pastoral ministry. In crisis, loss, grieving, unexpected transitions, and times of special need and celebration, this is a legitimate expectation. Life's most significant moments—birth, marriage, baptism, and death, among others—are prime opportunities for pastoral ministry. However, congregants mistakenly believe that this kind of care should characterize most of the pastor's ministry, seeing themselves as the primary beneficiaries. Quite often, pastors do little to correct this notion and are reluctant to equip and share ministry with the laity.

The gap between clergy and laity tends to create a perception that pastors and pastoral candidates should somehow be free of the imperfections, blemishes, and baggage from past history that we expect in others. The reality, however, is that those who prepare for this vocation have the same range of strengths, weaknesses, struggles, questions, personality types, and emotional and spiritual maturity that we find within the church as a whole. In other words, God calls very human people to pastoral work. Since the success of pastoral ministry depends on a clear understanding of personal strengths, weaknesses, opportunities, and expectations, congregations and educational institutions often work together to help individuals explore their calling in a number of ways.

One method to help people think through their calling is the use of various types of testing—personality, psychological, spiritual giftedness, among others. Moreover, since no one can step back far enough to have an uncontaminated view of self, a healthy process involves feedback in community from peers and professionals, personal reflection, mentoring, and counseling as needed. We are all a mixed bag of wholeness and brokenness, so these processes help pastoral candidates identify areas of personal, psychological, and spiritual strength, as well as weakness and vulnerability.

One obvious advantage of spotting vulnerabilities early is that wounds and brokenness experienced in life can result in failure in pastoral ministry and significant suffering and loss. A youth pastor, who was excellent with teens but struggling in his marriage, acknowledged that ministry had become his mistress. This was a major factor contributing to his wife's filing for divorce. Several years later he was able to own the brokenness, addictive behaviors, and poor choices that resulted in ministry failure. On the surface he seemed successful, and some were helped by his ministry; but many more suffered long-term ill effects from his unresolved issues. Those who have the opportunity to work through deep wounds before entering pastoral duties often have great insight and a deep commitment to ministering to others who suffer in similar ways.

Another reason to help pastoral candidates better understand their strengths and weakness is that congregations frequently have a distorted image of the ideal pastor. When pastors attempt to live up to unrealistic congregational expectations about their abilities or personality type, it often leads to disappointment and a sense of failure. A senior pastor of a megachurch was an extremely effective communicator in the pulpit but very introverted in personal relationships. Because he seemed comfortable in front of large crowds, people assumed he was extroverted, and he tried to live up to that expectation. However, in small groups and social settings he was obviously miserable. Congregants misinterpreted his behaviors, labeling him to be unloving, uncaring, and uninterested in them. If he had revealed his introversion initially and helped his congregants to understand that God calls and uses all different personality types, the result might have been very different.

No ideal personality type or skill set exists for pastors. Some effective pastors are more intuitive; others work from the senses. Some act based on feelings, while others rely heavily on reason. Whether task oriented with a focus on accomplishing goals or relationally oriented with a love for the communal journey, problem solvers or visionary thinkers or doers, there is a place in pastoral ministry for those who are called. One rapidly growing congregation did not understand the value of diverse abilities and gifts and continually tried to coerce their pastor to exhibit gifts and skills he would never have. Church members filled the elder board with critical observers who identified pastoral problems inaccurately. The pastor and his wife were depressed and ready to leave. Over time and with outside help, the situation was redeemed; but it exemplified intolerance for differences and the results of trying to impose unrealistic expectations. When pastoral candidates have a clear picture of their gifts, abilities, and personality, the temptation to make themselves fit congregational expectations is diminished. An honest appraisal of strengths and weaknesses early in the process helps pastoral candidates avoid common pitfalls later on.

PREPARATION IN THE ACADEMY

While the academy frequently assists those called to pastoral ministry to recognize their gifts, talents, and personal characteristics, it is most directly involved with the theological side of ministerial training. This theological core is essential, since pastoral ministry must always be grounded in participation in God's kingdom and its values. Unless these kingdom values are adopted by pastors, ministry can be co-opted by cultural pressures, faddish trends, or practices and strategies that reflect worldviews alien to Christianity.

The theological area of most direct application to pastoral ministry is, as one might expect, pastoral theology, which focuses on a theologically sound understanding of the role and practice of ordained ministry. Since pastoral ministry centers on proclamation of the word, administration of the sacraments, and equipping laity for ministry, a pastoral theology curriculum will include preparation for preaching and teaching, organization and administration, and sacramental practices. Pastoral theology also helps students develop professional skills and practices necessary in the church and the world, where increased specialization is expected. This includes preparation for counseling, generational ministries, evangelism, global ministries, and specialized equipping ministries (e.g., camping or sports ministry). Studying cultural contexts, human and ethnic diversity, languages, urban issues, and other topics provides a deeper understanding of the nature and practice of ministry. Ministry internship experiences are laced into the fabric of education to provide real time learning on site and through case studies in the classroom. The congregation plays a key role at this point in the educational process, as both student and congregation learn about pastoral ministry together.

In addition to studying pastoral and practical theology, students are exposed to a broad background in related theological disciplines. They are trained in how to understand, interpret, and teach the Bible. Courses in systematic theology help pastoral candidates learn to think theologically and to teach others to do so as well. Historical theology and church history provide a broader understanding of God's work in history and how the ideas, practices, and sacramental traditions of their own denomination fit into that history. Study in philosophy and ethics helps future pastors to develop a Christian worldview and to better understand other worldviews.

Typically, students ask why all of this study is necessary. It would be instructive for these students to speak with current pastors who entered ministry with little or no academic training and return later, realizing how much they still need to know. One pastor with limited educational preparation experienced numerical growth in his ministry, but recognized that he did not sufficiently understand the ministry of God and the needs of his people. He discovered that he had to address daily congregational issues from a clear biblical understanding, or discussions between him and his people simply became power plays. Instead of guiding them through scripture to appropriate applications, he found himself dictating or coercing responses, which resulted in stalemate and resistance. Since he had not developed skills in reflection and facilitating reflection in others, he found himself mandating belief, and this created friction.

Sometimes the congregation questions why all this educational training is necessary. Congregants, following our culture's desire for tools and strategies that address external behaviors, often place more value on result-oriented practices than theological reflection. The danger of this cultural influence can be illustrated by the case of a highly visible, well-known contemporary religious and political activist, who became a national lightning rod for several culturally divisive issues. As his support base increased his power and influence, the theological discussion of the issues diminished and was replaced by strong emotions and rigid convictions. Church members were caught up in their association with someone who wielded such power and influence. The ability of the pastor and his local congregation to bring a Christian perspective to these issues was lost in the process.

In both cases above, deep problems might have been avoided by the development of an integrated theology of ministry. A good theological education provides a Christian counterweight to strong cultural forces that can drive a pastor's choices. Education creates a gap between stimulus and response, event and reaction. In this gap, a pastor can reflect theologically and recognize and evaluate the many elements involved in a situation. It requires skills and confidence in God to stop and reflect before responding. Pastoral theology is designed to provide the skills and intentionality that will lead a pastor to place confidence in God. Without such a solid foundation, a pastor's calendar and work can easily be shaped by tasks that deflect attention from central pastoral responsibilities and rely on pragmatic methods divorced from theological values.

THE CALLING TO A CONGREGATION

Pastoral education is not, of course, an end in itself. The goal is ministry, and most pastors exercise their ministry within a congregational setting. The means by which pastors are called to congregational ministry differs. Some congregations have pastors who are appointed by denominational leadership; others call their own pastors. All churches desire a pastor who fits their perceptions of the role, matches their culture, and ministers to them in ways they deem most important.

The process of joining pastor and congregation together is similar to marriage, a covenantal union blessed by God. Prior to this commitment, each side learns as much as they can about the other, matching their discoveries against their needs and expectations. However, because the prospective pastor desires a place to minister and congregations are often anxious to find a pastor, important issues may be overlooked. In consequence, it is not uncommon after an initial honeymoon period for some of the concerns and tensions, dropped for the sake of the relationship, to begin to surface. At this point, each side's commitment is tested.

One congregation, hurt badly by previous failings in the pastor-congregational relationship, found a new pastor who had previously been successful to lead them. They welcomed him and gave him total authority to lead them, but after two years the relationship ended. Many had changed their initial view of the new pastor as savior to viewing him as arrogant. The rules had changed in the relationship. When they were hurting, they sought a healer, but when the healing was complete, the healer came to be seen as a dominator. In pastoral transitions, laity often seek someone with strengths where the former pastor was weak. Over time, this swinging of the leadership-style pendulum produces significant instability in the life of the church. Once again, we can see why congregations and educational institutions have traditionally worked together closely. Ideally pastoral candidates will draw on their time of exploration and education to gain a realistic picture of what ministry strengths and limitations they possess and what types of ministry best suit their gifts.

THE PASTOR AS AGENT OF TRANSFORMATION

When a pastor and congregation are joined, a new pastor finds herself faced with a number of issues. We will look at two common challenges of pastoral

ministry to show how academic training provides a background for addressing actual questions at the same time that the pastor's experience within a
congregation provides a context where learning continues.

First, pastors need to assess congregations and lead them to growth and
transformation. Continuing transformation is an assumption of the Christian faith, on both the individual and the congregational level. Therefore, the
pastor's role includes questioning why things are the way they are and facilitating congregational development. During the first year especially, a new
pastor will observe patterns that will be obscured after acclimating to the
church's culture. Initiating an evaluation can be threatening to the congregation, which wants the pastor to accept them unconditionally. There is an
ongoing tension between acceptance and change that pastors must work to
maintain.

The congregational evaluative process is discussed frequently during
a student's academic preparation. Students learn how to apply scripture,
church tradition, experience, and reason to questions of transformation.
They have thought through practical theology methods that seek to in-
fuse church practice with kingdom values. Students also familiarize
themselves with demographic studies and other tools to identify the behaviors, interests, and preferences of the community. In addition, they
nurture a discerning spirit open to God's leadership and lordship. This
preparation is helpful, but learning is embedded when students, faced
with concrete situations in a real congregation, have to put all these skills
into practice.

Congregations, like individuals, are creatures of habit. Research indicates that up to 80 percent of our behavior can be classified as habit. Habits
and traditions have an important role. If we had to decide anew each day
how we would dress, brush our teeth, or drive to work, we would have little time or energy left for important challenges. The same is true for congregations. Nevertheless, we are also aware that destructive and wasteful
habits become entrenched alongside good ones. This is where the role of
the pastor comes in. While pastors must facilitate the transformation of un-
productive habits into God-honoring patterns, they often forget how
painful change can be for the congregation. Change may result from providing new information and insight, but responses to the call for change are
frequently emotional. Fear, anger, grief, confusion, and more come into play
when pastors initiate change.

Remember, habit and the emotions that accompany it are part of the
outer ring of the transformation model we used earlier. Resistance is per-

ceived in this outer realm of values and behaviors, creating a strong temptation for pastors to address resistance by applying pragmatic methods based on business models with theological footnotes rather than theological method with business footnotes. Pastors are tempted to substitute the image of a CEO for the biblical model of the shepherd.

One of the reasons we focused on a transformation model at the beginning of the chapter is that congregational transformation parallels individual transformation; lives become transformed by moving from the inner story outward toward behaviors and habits. Just as individuals are confronted with their conflicts and sinfulness in the first act of the divine drama, congregations need to recognize their failings, tensions, and missed opportunities. In the second scene God is revealed to his people in Christ. He engages in the conflict, intervening through his Spirit. When a congregation cooperates with God in this engagement, the third scene of transformation occurs. Embracing the activity of the Spirit provides congregations with the resources and motivation for change and resolution.

The real difference between the theological model of transformation above and more pragmatic methods is that the latter tend to focus on changing circumstances, activities, and behaviors, while the theological model focuses on changing us at the core of our being—at the level of our story. Scripture and experience reveal that believers tend to break into this drama, taking things back into their own hands, because they do not like the result or because they believe God does not hear or care. When Christ-followers allow themselves to be changed, the drama recurs. As people change, new conflict and unsettledness provide further opportunities for transformation. This is the pattern of God in history with his people.

This theological model also helps us understand the logic of the three basic functions of pastoral ministry—proclaiming the word, administering the sacraments, and equipping laity. The proclamation of the word keeps us grounded in the story by reminding us that transformational change, not the complacency of habit, is the Christian norm. Proclamation of the story is mirrored in a concrete way through the sacraments, which remind us of our sin and the means by which God has provided for our salvation and transformation. The goal is for the pastor to help congregants engage in ministry themselves. This all points toward a Christian life viewed as a journey rather than a destination already achieved. For this reason, the academy teaches a pastor to serve people and model life for them in a way that normalizes ongoing transformation. In essence the pastor shepherds people in the rehabiting of heart and life.

MINISTRY TO BROKENNESS AND MINISTRY
TOWARD WHOLENESS

A second inherent tension in congregational ministry involves the twofold mission of the church. Christians are called to foster growth and maturity for believers, what we will call ministry toward wholeness. At the same time, ministries of brokenness—reaching out to humanity's emotional, physical, social, and spiritual problems and sin—are also necessary. As the church brings growing believers together with those needing redemption and healing, ministry becomes very complicated. Some churches focus on a strong discipleship ministry but neglect reaching out to the hurting, except perhaps through support of distant missions. Other churches focus on meeting social needs and conversion, but without discipleship. The church focused on wholeness might fear contamination by unrepentant sinners or might not know how to live with the problems brought in by those in need. Addressing brokenness, however, is time consuming and resource intensive. Without a sufficient emphasis on wholeness and discipleship, congregations will not have the resources for ministries to brokenness.

To succeed in providing a necessary balance between these ministries, pastors need to prepare laity to disciple and heal. This equipping can only occur in an environment where wholeness and the ongoing transformation of life is a norm that is woven into the fabric of church life. Maturing Christians need to be equipped to accept, love, and patiently nurture those who come with deep needs and suffering. If transformation is normal, those who suffer and need redemption will see it in action and desire the change. If it is not, brokenness often becomes the norm, leading to all kinds of internal community struggles. The ability to integrate faith and practice theologically, embracing personal wholeness and brokenness while leading others, is a prerequisite for pastoral ministry. Shepherding those with deep needs mandates a life that models spiritual well-being and calls others to a lifestyle of ongoing transformation.

SPECIALIZED PASTORAL MINISTRIES

To this point we have looked at pastoral ministry from the perspective of the single-pastor model, which is still a common paradigm. However, a young pastor is increasingly likely to have a specialized ministry as a member of a pastoral team. In this context it is necessary to maintain a strong, trusting team that allows each pastor to focus on a specific subgroup within the church. The pastor, in this case, preaches the word, celebrates sacraments, and equips laity within a specific population—youth, children, different adult age groups, small groups, and men's or women's ministries. Increasingly, these areas have further diversified to include sports outreach, urban ministries, counseling, finances, administration, visitation, special needs, ethnic ministries, assimilation, and many more.

Educational institutions have responded to the growing diversity of ministries by offering courses in these specialized areas, and this training can be very useful. However, the emphasis of pastoral education remains on helping students develop a broad-based theology of ministry that is able to flex with changes. There are several reasons for this. The first is simply that pastors are required to develop many skills. Beyond preaching, sacramental celebration, and lay equipping, today's pastor is expected to be proficient in administration, counseling, conflict management, project management, team building, new leadership styles, postmodernism, generational issues, multiple worship styles, outreach, future trends, finance management, technology, social and political issues, church-related legal issues, personnel issues, church-operated schools, demographic studies, and much more. A second reason for a broad-based approach is that pastors will frequently find themselves in specialized ministries they did not envision during their education. Finally, no school has the resources to offer specific courses or programs in all these ministry areas. This again brings us back to the partnership between the congregation and the academy. While the academy can provide a general theological and practical framework, much of the pastor's education occurs while in actual ministry settings.

BUT I'M NOT CALLED TO PASTORAL MINISTRY

The majority of those who read this chapter will never experience a call to pastoral ministry. Does that mean that you have just wasted a valuable chunk of time? I don't think so. In fact, if you are a Christian, this may be one of the most practical chapters you will read. After all, you are likely part of a congregation, and, as I have emphasized in this chapter, the congregation is a vital part of a pastor's life. It is not only the context in which most pastors work. The congregation is where pastors receive their call, go through a discernment of their gifts, and eventually exercise those gifts. If you are engaged in some type of ministry (as all Christians should be), your work within the kingdom will intersect with your pastor's. Unless all Christians have a clear picture of the nature and demands of pastoral ministry, the tensions mentioned throughout this book can hinder our efforts at outreach and discipleship.

The academy's primary role is to partner with congregations by equipping pastoral candidates who will then equip the laity for ministry. A large part of this task is helping both prospective pastors and congregations reflect on the goal they share—mutual participation in transformational ministry to the world. When the academy and congregations partner in this important goal, there are many reasons to be optimistic about the future health of the church community and the resulting ministry.

11

PRACTICAL THEOLOGY:
A BRIDGE ACROSS THE DIVIDE?

Paul Shrier and B. J. Oropeza

Scripture provides us with a story where Jesus finds himself in a difficult situation. He had been asked by Jewish leaders whether it was permissible for Jews to pay a tax to Caesar, and, for reasons we will outline later, his answer had to be carefully crafted, because a lot was riding on it. In shaping his response, Jesus was aware of several things. He knew that many Jews of his day resented living under the thumb of Roman conquerors. There were, however, Jews who benefited from this rule. In light of this sociological background, Jesus recognized that his answer could provoke conflicting responses. He also had at his disposal certain truths about God's nature and God's expectations for his followers. What Jesus did not have was a crib sheet that told him exactly what he should do in this very unique situation.

Our experience frequently parallels that of Jesus. We are confronted with situations where we need to apply what we know about our faith to a concrete problem or question. While scripture is certainly our foundational authority, it does not provide a set of pat, off-the-rack answers to every conceivable situation a Christian will encounter. This is true even when we follow the advice of previous chapters, faithfully considering the literary genre, translation issues, and historical and social context, as well as the canonical context of the passages we are reading. So what do we do when we need to make wise decisions in cases where ready-made answers are not available? In such situations, it is useful to have at our disposal a variety of thought structures or *methods* that remind us to carefully consider the important historical and current factors as we craft responses that faithfully express God's will. This is where practical theology comes into play.

Practical theology is concerned with both thinking and acting according to God's purpose in all aspects of daily life by carefully considering the

Bible and resources springing from it while keeping one eye on what is happening in our daily world. Because of this, it is particularly well suited to create collaborative opportunities for the congregation and the academy. This chapter will outline one simple method of practical theology that can harness the potential of a congregation–academy alliance. This method provides one possible framework for incorporating theological disciplines to make sound Christian judgments and to develop effective action strategies consistent with these judgments.

Some caveats are in order before we develop this particular approach to "thinking Christianly." First, this particular practical theology method is one of many possible practical theology approaches. Second, the usefulness of the academic disciplines outlined previously is not limited to their application within this method. Finally, this approach is only valuable when the love, wisdom, and faith of a Christian community are embodied in it. It is not intended to be used by a disinterested observer, if such a person even exists, to obtain a wise Christian outcome. This structure can, however, assist Christian communities as they strive to grow in love, faith, and wisdom. In addition, it is a useful starting point for re-integrating the congregation and the academy.

"DECIDE"

The old saying, "A long journey begins with a single step" contains a relevant truth. Christians begin integrating Christian beliefs into areas of life that were previously uninformed by Christian faith and improve their Christian practice in other areas of life by taking an initial step. The DECIDE process allows an individual Christian or a Christian community to determine the direction of their journey and to make concrete initial steps. It then assists Christians with the essential process of adjusting their trajectory to arrive at their final destination. The letters in the DECIDE acronym help us to remember the following six-step procedure: First, we carefully Describe the situation. Second, we Explore alternative explanations for the current state of affairs. Third, and the pivotal point for Christians, we Consider Christian teachings and perspectives that may provide guidance in these circumstances. Fourth, and often neglected, we consider how alternative explanations from science, history, the social sciences and other sources can Inform or even Integrate with our Christian teachings. Fifth, we Develop new guidelines and actions. Finally, we Evaluate the outcome, considering intended and unintended consequences.

This method is described below by briefly introducing each step of the DECIDE process. The process is then used to consider how Christians who are entering their careers ought to view and respond to globalization. The discussion of globalization is a summary of an actual class exercise that was undertaken in one of our previous practical theology classes.

Describe the Situation

The first step in this process is to describe, clearly and carefully, the present practices that are causing concern or tension. In practical theology the term *practice* refers to actions that have become so common that people automatically perform them when appropriate circumstances arise. Practices, rather than being one of several options, become the default response in a given situation. Practices may be unique to an individual, to a specific age group, or to a subgroup within society. Such subgroups would include but not be limited to churches and even whole denominations.

Practices need to be described, because their commonness often causes us to overlook the justifications for their use and their positive and negative impacts on various members of society. Academic disciplines such as sociology, psychology, organizational management, and macroeconomics can be employed to describe a practice accurately. As an example, this book's Old Testament chapter reminded Western readers that our prosperity, while a blessing from God, is not God's required response to our Western piety and obedience. Instead, our blessing from God carries the responsibility of actively working to meet the material needs of those who are less fortunate. This critique seeks to shed light on the extent to which Christians have uncritically adopted Western consumption patterns.

But have Christians actually been co-opted by our society's consumerism? To describe what is really happening it is worthwhile to consider recent studies of American earning and spending patterns. Also, are there studies that compare Christian consumption patterns with those of the whole society? Informal surveys of students or congregation members, examining consumption messages in popular television shows and movies, evaluating the themes of popular Christian books, considering over a period of time the themes in the sermons preached at your church, and other forms of careful observation all work together to describe actual American Christian consumption patterns. These same tools can be used to consider many other contemporary issues.

As another example, I asked my practical theology class to consider a Christian response to globalization from their perspective as college students who will soon be looking for jobs. They were given several articles and some Bible passages to aid them in crafting a response. They began by describing structural changes in the American job market resulting from globalization. As a group the class identified three major factors that would affect their work opportunities. First, they recognized that a segment of American jobs requiring advanced degrees in accounting, information technology, and other fields were being outsourced to emerging countries like India. Second, they identified the significant immigration of Hispanic peoples into the United States as an additional source of labor who are competing for existing jobs. Finally, they discovered that rapid increases in productivity have lead to largely jobless economic recovery and expansion. Once students named these three specific trends in the American job market, several of them recognized that they felt less anxious about their future careers. The description process had surfaced and concretely described changes in the economy that had been a source of anxiety for soon-to-be graduates. Once specific trends were identified, students felt ready to evaluate these changes and respond productively.

You might say, "This sounds too difficult. Why is it necessary to put this much thought and effort into describing our current practices?" There are a few responses to this concern. First, while the description process sounds daunting, you will find it simpler in practice. Second, the results are often intriguing, encouraging us to undertake further research. Third, even when we have time constraints, a limited effort to describe a situation accurately will often identify its key components. Sometimes a simple initial description reveals there is no problem with current actions. Alternatively, a limited initial effort may reveal that the situation is more complex than we thought.

The following analogy may be helpful: If your doctor thought you had breast cancer or a heart problem, would you prefer her to make a superficial diagnosis or to use all the tools at her disposal to carefully describe the nature and extent of your illness? I know that I would want my doctor to use whatever tools were available to make the most accurate diagnosis possible. Then I can have more confidence in the suggested treatment and the prognosis. A clear description of current circumstances is part of solid practice in every field of endeavor, including Christian responses to other people and circumstances.

Explore Alternative Explanations

After carefully describing the action or issue in question, we need to consider how these actions have been or can be evaluated. The first part of this exploration involves considering the investigator's views. Why are we even concerned with this situation? What are our social and theological positions? How might these impact our evaluations? In our New Testament chapter Reeves and Waters showed that 1 Corinthians was concerned with our selfish tendencies, including the tendency to slant our appraisals to meet our own needs and to make us look good. To better evaluate any situation, then, we must begin by examining our own position and motives.

Once we have come as clean as we are able about our prejudices, several questions can be explored. Consider the case described in the pastoral theology chapter where a congregation is not growing because they believe evangelism is the job of the religious professionals, that is, their pastoral staff. Evaluating the history of the congregational beliefs on this matter would be a place to start an evaluation. Historically, what has the congregation been taught about the pastor-congregation relationship and roles? How has the congregation related to their community in the past? Has it been taught to remain separate from the world? Also, it helps to consider who benefits and who suffers from this practice of letting the pastors evangelize. Further, in what ways does this particular practice mirror societal practices, such as our current societal movement toward professional specialization? Also, what constraints does this model place upon the church and the community? How does it shape the role of the pastors and the congregants? These and other questions would allow us to better explain what is really happening. It allows us to discover blind spots and latent opportunities for change. It also gives everyone a chance to be understood.

When my practical theology students described globalization effects on the job market, they evaluated the source and significance of outsourcing, new Spanish-speaking immigrant labor, and rapid productivity gains. They identified several factors that require a specifically Christian response. First, they learned that outsourcing information technology jobs is annually creating several hundred thousand jobs in India. These jobs directly and indirectly raise the standard of living for millions of people who desperately need this help. The students discovered a similar positive impact for many of the Spanish-speaking immigrants entering the United States while family members remain in Latin America. Thus, from a Christian perspective, both of these changes are helping people meet basic needs for food, shelter, health care, and education in less-developed nations and lower-income families. Finally, they discovered that productivity improvements have increased the number of men and women who lose their jobs and must accept lower-paying, entry-level jobs. A result of this is job insecurity that creates a culture of uncertainty among established Americans. This uncertainty increases anxiety levels and may lead to fear-driven health and family problems. They determined that as Christians we ought to consider how we can alleviate this climate of anxiety and fear.

Consider Christian Perspectives

This particular step considers what happened in the Bible and church history that might relate to our current concerns. We also consider what theological constructs can say about our concerns. What Christian resources can guide our current beliefs and behaviors? Some questions that focus on the Bible might include: What Old Testament and New Testament stories seem to be dealing with similar problems? What does the teaching, poetry, and wisdom literature contribute? What are the historical and situational contexts of these texts? Also, how have these texts been employed historically to develop Christian practices? Systematic and historical theology might consider these questions: What theological doctrines relate to this problem? Which theologians have discussed it? What ethical teachings have dealt with these issues?

Christian sources should be broadly explored initially. As an example, my wife (a biologist) and I wrote a paper discussing a Christian perspective on human embryonic stem cell research. When we came to this stage in our process, we considered every Bible passage we could think of, without censoring our imagination. Some passages, like the poetic description of God knitting us in our mother's womb in Psalm 139, were obvious. Others, like the story of Solomon's judgment that a baby be cut in half to appease the two women who claimed to be the baby's mother, were not. Ultimately we did not use the second story. Initially, however, we wanted to consider anything that might be relevant.

Ideally, several specific Bible stories, theological doctrines, church history events, and other Christian resources can be identified that relate to a situation. The number of resources that you identify and use will depend on the relative importance of your situation. While I might spend an hour considering how I ought to behave as a Christian when I order food at a restaurant, I would spend considerably more time considering what it means to provide my children with a Christian education and upbringing. Once we have identified appropriate resources, we can consider how they support our current behaviors, how they call into question our current attitudes and responses, and how we might be able to craft totally new responses to a situation.

I asked my students who were developing a response to the globalization of the job market to consider two New Testament passages. I knew that these would challenge some of their preconceptions. The first passage was the story of the good samaritan (Luke 10:25–37). As expected, my students recognized that the Hispanic immigrants, the Indian information technology workers, and the managers who were trying to maintain their competitive position were our neighbors. Students who were interested in social justice enthusiastically embraced the Christian standard of supporting improvements for the underprivileged, but they maintained a suspicion of businesses that were making large productivity gains. Meanwhile, my students who were business oriented also supported the productivity gains and the improved lifestyles of the workers who benefited.

This is the second passage that I asked them to consider:

> The first is, "Hear, O Israel: The Lord our God, the Lord is one; you shall love the Lord your God with all your heart, and with all your soul, and with all your mind, and with all your strength." The second is this, "You shall love your neighbor as yourself." There is no other commandment greater than these. (Mark 12:29–31)

Some students did not recognize that some tension exists between this passage and their interpretation of the story of the good samaritan. Others, however, recognized that this passage bases neighborly love on a previous self-love. In the context of globalization, self-love creates the responsibility for Christians to seek their own well-being as well as the well-being of their neighbors. A Christian response to globalization required students to seek the good of their own family as well as the good of their neighbors. This scripture-based view of a mutual love ethic rather than a simplistic sacrificial love ethic affirms global employment that benefits others while also asserting the right of American Christians to seek and obtain meaningful employment. The dangers of dualism recognized in chapter 7 are avoided through embracing this mutual love ethic: the physical needs of North, South, and Central Americans, as well as those of Indians, are placed on an equal footing. We avoid a false division between providing for the physical needs of others while denying our own physical needs to meet our spiritual needs or obligations. The mutual love ethic maintains a balance, because it does not allow us to idolize work or validate storing up wealth for its own sake.

Inform/Integrate Christian Resources and Alternative Explanations

We have not completed an accurate evaluation of a situation once we have considered biblical, theological, and social science or other perspectives on the topic. In order to craft Christian behaviors, we need to consider how Christian resources relate to insights gained from other sources.

At the outset of this chapter we identified a dilemma that Jesus faced when he was asked by the Pharisees (a Jewish religious party loyal to traditions related to Jewish law) and the Herodians (a party loyal to King Herod, who was essentially a puppet ruler for Tiberius Caesar) if it was lawful to pay taxes to Caesar (Matthew 22:15–22; Mark 12:13–17; Luke 20:20–26). They flattered Jesus, saying that they knew he would answer them truthfully regardless of consequences, pressuring Jesus to give a candid response.

Their question was legitimate even though their motives were not: Mark indicates that they intended to trap Jesus (Mark 10:13), likely to provide grounds for accusing Jesus of treason. The tension in their question was that the Jews lived under Roman rule. For Roman tribute the Jews had to pay one silver coin, called a denarius, every year. Such a tax collection led to a riot in 6 C.E., when devout Jews protested against Rome. Rome subdued the uprising, but strong resentment over taxes persisted within the community. If Jesus agreed with paying taxes, he would be labeled a traitor by the Pharisees; if he disagreed, the Herodians would deliver him up to Roman authorities for judicial punishment as seditionist.

Jesus' answer indicated that he had accurately *described* and *assessed* the situation; he was aware of their hidden agenda—more than a simple question about taxes was at stake. It arose more from political and religious affiliations than an honest attempt to get at the truth. Moreover their question was *halakhic* in nature; it concerned the Jewish law: They asked "is it *lawful*" to pay taxes to Caesar?

Jesus would have also *considered* the Jewish scriptures relevant in this situation; he could have appealed directly to Jewish law. He could have responded that the image on the coin was idolatrous, reverencing another god besides the God of the Old Testament, particularly if the coin's inscription bore the title the "son of the deified Augustus" for Tiberius Caesar. However, evaluating Jewish scripture in light of the devious motives of his questioners, he avoided this answer. It would only aggravate the current tension; he would be jeopardizing either his own safety or his reputation as a wise teacher of the Jewish people. Given his circumstances, a reevaluation of Old Testament law was in order, so he implemented a new model addressing tribute to the God-dishonoring political structure of Rome *without* dishonoring God. He asked that a silver coin used for paying taxes be brought to him and then asked whose image it bore. The Pharisees and Herodians said "Caesar's." Jesus then replied, "Give back to Caesar the things that are Caesar's and the things of God to God." His answer was so profound that his enemies were left speechless!

The creative answer Jesus gave remained loyal to Old Testament tradition. Although he recognized paying tribute to the Roman government, he suggested a greater duty remained. Humanity, which bears the image of God rather than Caesar (Genesis 1:26–27), has an obligation to obey God. And one's duty to God is different from one's duty to the government. In this manner not only did Jesus protect himself from wrongful accusation, but he also provided a constructive explanation that would help both the Herodians and Pharisees recognize their obligation to please God. He revealed the heart of the issue without falling into the trap of giving a black-and-white, is-it-lawful-or-unlawful answer.

As Jesus did above, we need to consider and use appropriately our Christian resources in light of other societal considerations. It is helpful when examining relevant Bible passages and comparing them to science, history, and social science responses to ask the following four questions: Where do our Bible texts and theological teachings conflict with current societal evaluations of this situation? Where are these two sources of information and wisdom independent of each other? Where can they provide a dialogue that improves our response? And finally, where can we integrate current scientific, historical, sociological, anthropological, and other evidence into our Bible- and theology-inspired response to a situation? This integration requires careful analysis, following guidelines such as those discussed in the philosophy chapter of this book. Jesus exhibits this depth of thinking, some might call it wisdom, in many of his controversies recorded in the Gospels.

My students contextualized the passages on the love of God, mutual love, and neighborly love to create new Christian responses to globalization for future job opportunities. In general, students suggested that we take the time to learn about other cultures and about the material situations of people in other countries. They also suggested that we look at downsizing and outsourcing from several angles, attempting to measure the good as well as the harm that occurs. These students also emphasized that they need to become good learners to respond creatively and flexibly to rapidly changing work environments. They talked about excelling in their professions so in the future they will be able to bring Christian love into the equation in business decisions. Finally, they talked about actively meeting the needs of those who had lost their jobs and about how their churches and other social assistance groups might provide support.

Develop New Guidelines and Practices

Once Christian doctrines and practices have been explored and modern issues in the translation of these practices have been considered, the fifth step is to create new guidelines and practices that faithfully reflect Christian teachings. Questions that can be asked while developing these practices include: How do they further the kingdom of God? Who benefits from these practices? How do they benefit? What obligations are created? For whom? How ought these new practices be communicated and implemented? What can be done to make these transitions as smooth as possible? How can the actual results of these practices be measured or identified once these changes have been made? Presumably, new practices will change positively the quality of life for individuals, their families, the community, and others who are impacted by the process. As this occurs, individuals will become open to further change, and this process can be repeated.

My students responded to globalization with several innovative ideas. First, almost all of my students indicated that they were going to learn Spanish—several made plans to change their remaining university course selections to include more Spanish courses. Other students decided to become involved in mentoring programs, either formal or informal, to work with new immigrants and to learn more about other cultures. Many students also decided to study advanced communication skills so they would be marketable in a variety of fields as the job market evolved. Finally, those students who planned to go into full-time ministry recognized that a significant part of their ministry would focus on assisting families harmed by rapid economic change.

Evaluate the New Actions

Whenever we change our behaviors our new actions have consequences. Some of these consequences are intended, while others are unintended. This stage of the DECIDE process recognizes that adjustments will be required when begin new programs, habits, and behaviors. When we first institute changes we ought to write them in sand, not in stone. In other words, if we institute them with the idea that they will need to be adjusted, our long-term results will improve. The evaluation step of this process involves quickly going through the whole procedure again, recognizing what you have done and how it has worked.

CONCLUSION

This chapter has presented one practical theology model as a structure for integrating academic disciplines with congregational concerns. When individual Christians make important decisions or when churches determine their direction, detailed use of this process will give them innovative decisions that they can implement with confidence. We have heard throughout this book that our vocation is not just our career. Our vocation is how we live every aspect of our lives. This includes all of our moment-by-moment, day-by-day choices. Nowhere in the Bible did we read Jesus say, "Take up your cross and follow me with the following exceptions." Christians may better follow Christ moment by moment if they are willing to internalize the essential elements of this or any practical theology method. For example, as we hurry to work we might remember to ask ourselves, "What am I doing right now as I speed to work? How anxious am I? What am I doing to my body and mind? How am I treating my life and the lives of others? What have I heard about worry and speeding on *Dr. Phil* and *60 Minutes*? Didn't I see a *Seinfeld* episode that ridiculed my behavior? What does the Bible say that might relate to my anxious feelings or even my speeding? How does this compare with what I remembered from *Oprah* or Jerry and Kramer? What should I be doing, and what will I do now?" Yes, this example sounds somewhat artificial. However, the main idea is valid. Practical theology is a discipline that actively works to develop means by which Christians can reflect on their daily practices. Many valuable insights have developed from these efforts. When Christians can learn to reflect on their behaviors from several angles, perhaps like looking at the many facets of a diamond, they will see both where they are doing well and where they can improve. Paul says in Philippians that he does not act as if he has reached the goal of serving Christ. Instead, he presses on toward perfection. He invites all Christians who are mature to do the same, following him as he follows Christ (3:12–17). Practical theology, with its ability to bridge the divide between good theory and good practice, is a valuable tool in understanding how we can more faithfully follow Jesus Christ.

12

BRIDGING PAST AND FUTURE

Amy Jacober and Steve Wilkens

Throughout this book we have come back frequently to the issue that initially motivated this project—the division that often exists between congregational ministries and the ministries provided by Christian universities. If both groups really want to make things work, and I think they do, we need to get our differences out on the table so we can confront them and work things out. When we talk about stress points between congregation and academy, it often boils down to something mentioned briefly in the first chapter: Congregations often think that universities are too liberal. It's not always clear what liberal means or what is wrong with it, but the charge generally expresses a fear that beliefs central to Christianity will be watered down so that we end up with something less than true Christianity. If Christians are going to worry about something, the concern that our faith could become a pale shadow of the real thing is certainly valid, so this is worth taking seriously.

As you have read through the various chapters, you may have run across ideas that seem a bit questionable, and for this reason you might be concerned that they express a type of liberalism. However, let us suggest an idea that might seem completely shocking to you. Some of the views outlined in the book may seem uncomfortable, not because they are too liberal, but because they are *too conservative*.

Hardly anyone today describes educational institutions, even Christian ones, as conservative, so the claim that the academy may make congregations nervous because it is too conservative probably needs a bit of explanation. "Conservative," in its most basic definition refers to a desire to conserve or preserve something. An academic conservative, then, wants to preserve whatever there is in the past, around the globe, within other disciplines, or from different perspectives that will help us understand where we are and make good decisions about where we go from here. Conservatives are rooted in the past, because they believe that, even though our circumstances may change rapidly, human nature is consistent. The basic questions, struggles, and issues concerning sin and salvation, good and evil, life and death, have remained throughout history. If this is the case, conserving our knowledge of the past, with all its problems, errors, and great ideas has the potential to keep us from making some very old mistakes and direct us toward some good resolutions.

If a conservative is defined as one who seeks to preserve the past, we are willing to bet that if you reread sections of this book that seem questionable and liberal, you will discover something interesting. You did not feel discomfort because the author seemed to be leaving out or watering down important beliefs. Instead, you may find that these sections suggest conserving and considering ideas that you believe are in error, misleading, confusing, problematic, and thus best forgotten. In many cases, you are right. Educational institutions preserve a lot of junk. They do this, however, because what may look like junk today may be tomorrow's treasure. Just ask anyone whose mom took a whole box of old baseball cards (including your Babe Ruth rookie card) to the dumpster. History reveals that our preservation of old ideas, traditions, memories, and movements often pays off. We just have to wait a while to see how it is going to work out.

Think back on the various chapters, and you will quickly see how conservative these different disciplines are. Those who wrote about philosophy and ethics encouraged us to use ideas from people like Kant and Descartes (both long dead) as an aid for thinking about issues like sexual fidelity and virtual reality. They have enlisted non-Christian thinkers like Aristotle (to help us think through what it means to be good) and Marx (to help us examine our tendencies to hide our selfish ambitions from ourselves).

Those who wrote about the Old Testament, New Testament, and biblical interpretation are also conservative in many ways. They help us maintain our memory of the original languages of scripture; the nonbiblical literature of the time of scripture; the traditions and cultures reflected in scripture; the Bible's various literary forms; the chronology, geography, and political and social structures of the biblical era; the processes by which oral traditions came to be written and collected; among other things. The motive behind the conservation of this knowledge is respect for scripture. If we truly want to know what it *says* to us today, we cannot get the most complete picture without knowing what it *said* within its original context.

Of course, Christians should be motivated to know what the Bible says to us today and how we can apply its message in a world that constantly changes. This is where the different types of theologies (historical, systematic, pastoral, practical theology, and theology of youth ministry) come into play. Each theological specialty makes us aware of how God's people have tried to make Christianity's message speak within different political, social, and cultural conditions throughout history. They conserve various theological traditions and ministry practices down through history (diachronic) as well as across the globe (synchronic) to remind us that Christianity has not been and is not now limited to any one ethnic group or cultural setting. This huge database of memory also provides resources to present the Christian story in a coherent and relevant way to different audiences and changing social structures. Finally, it is an expression of confidence that the Holy Spirit guides the church within history.

We have used quite a bit of space attempting to convince you that, according to the definition of conservative used here, the academy is a conservative place. (By the way, the fact that we put libraries, in which we keep our collective memories, in the middle of campuses is an example of this conservatism.) We now need to turn our attention to the second part of my thesis, that is, that a large part of the suspicion directed toward the academy results from this conservatism. To provide an example of how conservatism may contribute to a tension between the congregation and the academy, let us think about an issue that frequently divides Christians today—the ordination of women. Our intent here is not to solve the problem but to use it as an illustration of how conservatism might heighten tension between the academy and its constituents.

The first thing to notice is that most denominational groups or congregations believe that the matter of ordaining women is decided and settled. When the topic comes up in congregational settings, then, it is usually as a statement of position rather than an invitation for discussion. This is not to imply that congregations or denominations should not take a position on this question. In fact, it is necessary. A problem can arise, however, because even while many groups have staked out their position on women's ordination, this topic remains a lively conversation within the academy.

Does this mean that the academy is defiantly attempting to undermine its churches by entertaining ideas that many considered decided? This may be the case, but my experience is that this is one example of the academy's conservatism. It is the nature of a university to keep alternative viewpoints, different traditions, and minority interpretations in play to make sure we are always examining our positions. Another way of putting it is that the academy challenges positions by keeping other options alive and in front of us. When done properly, however, this challenge is not defiant, but a loving call to constantly reexamine questions of deep importance, precisely because the matters are so important. Nevertheless, challenges are always a bit unsettling.

A second reason for tension arising from the academy's conservative tendencies is data overload and confusion. When someone uses the academy's resources to investigate the question of the ordination of women, it will not take long before one feels completely overwhelmed. Preliminary research into the discussions of biblical passages and the culture of that era, the various movements and trends in the history of the church, different theological angles and positions, various practices around the world of Christianity, quickly leads to the feeling that someone could spend a whole lifetime studying nothing but this issue. All the different voices can create confusion, and confusion often creates problems. We generally feel like something is wrong unless we have clear-cut answers, and the deluge of information can often make it difficult to arrive at them. If students come out of college more confused than when they went in, what the use of that?

If the charge is that academics frequently create confusion, we plead guilty. However, there may be some mitigating circumstances. Confusion is never the goal of putting new ideas in front of people, even when it is part of the process. Herein lies part of the frustration felt by many folks in congregational settings. The academy is geared toward learning processes that stretch out over time. It assumes that students will go through periods of uncertainty about what they believe and what practices they should adopt. Congregations, on the other hand, need to make decisions and act. Confusion and uncertainty are thus viewed as obstacles to acting in decisive ways.

MAINTAINING A HEALTHY TENSION

If, as we have tried to argue, some of the tension created by the academy comes because its attempts to conserve a vast array of information and viewpoints generates challenges and confusion, how do we resolve this tension? Most of what we have said points toward a desire to do just that—resolve the tension—but let us suggest a slightly different way of looking at things. Maybe we should keep the tension in place, but make it a healthy tension rather than a destructive one. We have stated at points that, while congregation and academy share the goal of greater conformity with God's kingdom, the ways in which we work toward this differ. If we understand this tension in our methods and, at the same time, keep our common goal in view, we may have a constructive way to move forward together.

When we are at our best, Christian academics recognize that the point of our work is to bring us ever closer to a full and complete understanding and practice of the Christian faith. While we might have deep loyalties to certain theological traditions and denominational ties, we try to be very careful about equating them with absolute Christian truth. That is why we continually bring up different voices and traditions for re-examination. In other words, we challenge ideas in ways that often create a lot of confusion.

Sometimes these challenges and the resulting upheavals do slow things down. However, this process can generate useful change. If your church or denomination has been around for a while, it is likely that at some time in its history it has modified some basic doctrinal positions or practices. Many have done so on the very matter we are using as our example—the ordination of women. (Interestingly, the changes have gone both ways. Some groups that used to ordained women in the past no longer do so; others have changed to allow it.) The point is that, through prayerful thought and examination, Christians sometimes conclude that their beliefs and practices could conform more closely to the kingdom of God. By keeping alternative ideas before us, then, the academy can suggest correctives. It should also be noted that the academy does not simply conserve our memory of views that differ from our own tradition. It also preserves our understanding of our own denominational traditions and doctrines. Thus, for example, Quaker or Mennonite schools may remind their congregations about their tradition of nonresistance and call their churches back to those early views. Baptist universities, in turn, may remind their churches about the traditional Baptist reluctance to get too cozy with any particular political system. In short, part of the academy's obligation is to preserve its own specific theological heritage while also holding it up for examination and testing.

The congregation should keep up the tension on its side as well. It does well to remind the academy that, even in the midst of imperfect theology and practices, God is gracious enough to move his kingdom forward. Getting it all right and straight is not a requirement. The congregation also needs to remind the academy that the process of learning, while important, is not the ultimate goal. At some point, the university needs to recognize that its desire to conserve the past is intended to provide resources for the church in the future. If schools become too conservative, if they get lost in the past, they do not offer much direction. The question, then, is how we take this step out of the past and into the future God intends for the church.

MOVING INTO THE FUTURE

This is precisely what we have been trying to prepare you for—the future. The future will come; what you do with it will be your choice. Our desire is that you approach the throne of grace with boldness, wise as a serpent and gentle as a dove. Your time in classes was not meant to erase the faith built over years in your church; rather it was meant to strengthen it. The theological disciplines offer space to reflect, think, act, and grow. They constantly challenge one another all the while relying on one another. Theology (which, in the broadest sense of the word, comprises the full body of disciplines mentioned) does not and cannot exist apart from faith in Jesus Christ.[1] At the end of the day, each Christian academic within his or her specific discipline works from the position of faith. The authors you have read are not trying to tear down Christian beliefs; rather they are so passionately in love with Jesus and so confident in God's ability to withstand any questioning that theirs is a faith-seeking understanding.

DELIBERATE THOUGHT

We want to encourage you to be thinking Christians as well. Much has been done throughout history that is a blessing and encouragement. Unfortunately much has also been done in the absence of reflective thought for which we are now embarrassed and must repent. There is wisdom that comes not only with faith, but with humility, age, reflection, action, and thinking. We want you to be wise as a serpent. Each chapter has offered insight into this in one way or another. The nature of God and humanity, the meaning of life, and the position of evil have been among the many overarching themes introduced. Like many things, nuances may be lost on the first read. This conclusion will attempt to clarify how to move forward, how to carry your own faith-seeking understanding into the future.

    This idea of questioning and study is not new. In spite of what some churches think, the academy did not create the concept of studying one's faith to secure our livelihood or our vocational calling. You only have to go as far as Acts 17:16–34 to read of Paul engaged in conversation and proclamation with those in his day who wrestled with questions similar to our own. These same questions of the nature of God, the nature of humanity, the meaning of life, and the position of evil have dominated thought. The argument has been made that the academy is in reality trying to conserve or return the community of faith, the church, to her former position as a community of theologians. Theology wrestles with the questions of everyday life and afterlife. As an earlier chapter reminds us, when the church became formalized and universities were built, the study of theology gradually shifted away from the people and into the hands of a select few. In this we can catch a glimpse of the origin of the not-so-great divide. Remember, though, many have moved from their roots—many universities were built to train clergy. Up to that point, theology had always been practical. It had been intrinsically connected with everyday Christian living. In the eighteenth century Friedrich Schleiermacher was instrumental in articulating the relationship between theory and practice though even his focus remained primarily in the actions of the church and not everyday Christian living. Current theology has been undergoing a restoration of sorts. It is seeking to balance the conservation of our heritage while opening the way for continued conversations and questioning. It is not blasphemous for Christians to ask questions or to engage in dialogue. We do this, however, from a position of faith that should impact all we say and do. In fact, your faith should also impact all you say and do. This includes your activities here and now as well as your choices for the future. More on that in just a few paragraphs.

ROOTS AND WINGS

Our roots are important. Churches name fellowship halls after saints who contributed to the church community in significant ways. While a huge honor, it does not take long before the younger generation has no idea why it is Washington Hall or the Taylor Educational Building. Someone must intentionally pass on these stories to keep their significance alive. And so it goes with the relationship between the academy and the congregation. As you have read over and over again in previous chapters, the academy is not the congregation, nor is it trying to be. In its best moments, the Christian university recognizes and fulfills its unique role in the body of Christ. The academy reminds us of history, of statements made hundreds— if not thousands—of years ago and in unfamiliar places that still have an impact today. It also offers ways to interpret principles from days gone by, gives space for reflection, and attempts to create templates to be used in real-life situations.

A great heartache for many of us who teach is the struggle we have encouraging our fellow Christians to think. I know, it sounds crazy! As children, we accept being told what to do and, for the most part, what to think.

When we hit adolescence, those days of passively accepting instruction begin to disappear. We all have spent a great deal of time growing up and trying to prove that we are in charge of our own decisions and choices. Yet, when placed in a setting designed for learning, many revert to wanting to be told the answers. The academy is not here to brainwash anyone. The church is not alive today simply by doing what she has always done. Criticisms on both sides are often invalid and ill informed. Both the church and the academy are dynamic, and while ever moving forward, whether acknowledged or not, they stand on the shoulders of those who have come before.

We not only stand on the shoulders of those who came before, but we stand side by side as we support and hold one another up in the present. This is true both between the congregation and the academy and within the realm of each. Each academic discipline has clear distinctions but cannot be understood apart from the others. Theology requires a reading of scripture. Reading scripture requires both the Old and New Testaments. To correctly understand scripture hermeneutics must be taught (which by the way would not exist if we were not trying to read the Old and New Testaments). Philosophy wrestles with categorical questions in life often stemming from theological principles (whether realized or not) and sometimes vice versa. Ethics is a branch of philosophy that some view as the logical beginning point of theology. When we look at pastoral ministry and youth ministry, each a focused task of the church that has led to their existence as distinct disciplines, they both inform and are shaped by the other disciplines, ushering in further nuances. It always reminds me of the proverbial chicken and egg—which came first? It is difficult to tell which discipline existed first. (I will not even attempt to make that kind of claim here!) What I will say is that they are linked.

Not only are they linked to one another as academic disciplines, but they are linked within the church. By church I mean the lives of Christians, the community of people who follow Jesus Christ. The chicken and egg may help as a metaphor in illustrating that we cannot tell which came first, but it does nothing to explain their relation. The relationships of the disciplines within the Christian community and the academy are more like the facets of a rare and precious jewel. Sometimes they are adjacent to one another, sometimes not. Congregations must make decisions all the time. A decision about what time to begin, what songs to sing, to sprinkle or immerse for baptism, to support a local charity, or what kind of new carpet should be installed with the remodel. Each of these decisions is made by individuals or groups of individuals who ask tough questions (philosophy), seek guidance through prayer and scripture (Old and New Testament/ hermeneutics), try to understand the principles being drawn from scripture (theology) and their own traditions and past (history), and try to make moral decisions (ethics) about what exactly should be done (ministry). The entire process, when broken down into all of its facets, is comprised of the disciplines. This is not limited to the action of the formalized church by any means. Every day people make decisions in the same fashion. Decisions about whether to recycle (stewardship), to engage in certain recreational activities (piety), to volunteer (care for the poor), or to skip school or work to rest (laziness or Sabbath) comprise everyday praxis for Christians. Schleiermacher was correct to tie the disciplines with the church, but he did not go far enough. This has and continues to be corrected. In current times, practical theology is the voice calling specific attention to restore theology (in the broadest sense) back to its position within the daily life of all Christians.

VOCATION: MORE THAN A JOB

So you may be thinking, "Great. This is all fascinating, but what does this have to do with me?" Well, we'll tell you. All Christians are called by God. Called not necessarily for paid pastoral positions, but called to wrestle with the tough questions of life, to reflect on what you know in the context of your faith as you attempt to come to decisions that honor God. You are called to be a thinking Christian, wise as a serpent. You are called to think Christianly in all you do. What freedom comes with this news! You don't have to sacrifice your interest in engineering or marketing to be a pastor or missionary in a far-off land to honor God. You can honor God through faithful service as a biologist or musician, as a sportscaster or social worker. With great freedom, however, comes great responsibility. The responsibility part comes when you finally get it. When you understand that going to church on Sunday, tithing, and not cussing is not the measure of being a follower of Christ. It is when you take the time to do the work and learn how to think Christianly in all that you do. This is called your vocation.

    Vocation is one of those funny words that is misunderstood more often than not. Perhaps it would be best to begin with what it is not. As we noted in the opening chapter, vocation is not just a job; it is not even your career. It stems from the Latin *vocare,* meaning "to call." Your vocation is your calling. Unfortunately calling too has been misunderstood. For the Christian, we are called to act out God's reconciliation in this world. This includes our own relationship with Christ as well as how we choose to live this out, seeking and furthering the kingdom of God. Our vocation is not necessarily tied to what we do to earn a paycheck. It can be, but not necessarily. This is good news! Gone is the fear that if you do not discern the exact occupational calling for which God created you, you will not be in the center of the divine will and thus will derail God's perfect plan in your life and the world. God does place desires in our heart. God has created each of us in unique and beautiful ways. This is so basic to God's very nature that the great diversity in occupational choices is vital to our existence. This diversity is brought together in our common vocation, that of glorifying God in all we do.

This is not to say that we live out our vocation automatically. In fact, the sad truth is that many people become so consumed with the letter of the law, with living just right, that they miss the spirit of the law. God is equally pleased with the person who volunteers as an after-school tutor, landscapes a community college, or invents a new heart valve as long as each glorifies God in his or her field. You can even change your occupation and not abandon God, if you choose a job and accomplish what you were hired to do or alternatively find that it is a terrible fit and change. Throughout, if you continue to participate in your relationship with Jesus and his work of reconciliation in the world, your vocation has not changed. A vocation is a lifelong journey, not a one-time choice or event. God desires to be in a vibrant, living relationship with you in the everydayness of your life. This is the Christian calling.

A LASTING RELATIONSHIP

Faith and theology are inextricably linked. The church and the theological academy, too, are inextricably linked. Like most families, disagreements do occur. With the existence of disagreement comes a certain amount of trust or belief that the relationship is secure enough to weather the challenge. We are called to faith in the church. We are called to reflect on that faith and grow even more as a result of being in school. Academic disciplines provide tools that were never intended to remain cloistered within the ivory tower. These tools, as we have suggested, help us describe, explain, consider, integrate, and design our response to a broad array of issues that arise in our Christian walk. This process will use the biblical or historic disciplines and employ carefully crafted philosophical questions. Theology and ethics nuance and clarify our thinking to further develop a Christian perspective in the midst of our circumstances. Ministry is not a goal at the end. Instead, it is the focused process that happens along the way. Practical theology desires, even more it demands, the intentional conversation among and between the disciplines and daily living. You ask why it is important for you to study theology when you have no plans of becoming a pastor. It is even more important precisely because you have no plans of becoming a pastor. If you are a follower of Christ, you have a vocation that requires thinking Christianly. If you are a follower of Christ, it is your faith that should provide the motivation to do just such a thing. You have the privilege to have others on whose shoulders you will stand and beside whom you will walk as your faith seeks understanding. May you not neglect Jesus' call to be wise as a serpent and innocent as a dove.

NOTE

1. It should be mentioned that biblical and theological studies can occur apart from faith as religious studies. Religious studies often refers to the investigation of religious traditions and texts by someone outside the community of faith. Theology proper is done from within the community, therefore requiring and presupposing faith.

ABOUT THE CONTRIBUTORS

Heather Ann Ackley, Ph.D., is chair of Department of Theology and Philosophy and associate professor of theology at Azusa Pacific University.

John Culp, Ph.D., is professor of philosophy at Azusa Pacific University.

Steve Gerali, Ph.D., is associate professor of youth ministries and practical theology at Azusa Pacific University.

Amy Jacober, Ph.D., is assistant professor of practical theology and youth ministries at Azusa Pacific University.

Ralph P. Martin, Ph.D., is scholar in residence at Azusa Pacific University.

Dennis Okholm, Ph.D., is professor of theology at Azusa Pacific University.

B. J. Oropeza, Ph.D., is assistant professor of biblical studies at Azusa Pacific University.

Kara Powell, Ph.D., is assistant professor for youth and family ministry and executive director of the Center for Youth and Family Ministry at Fuller Theological Seminary.

Dick Pritchard, D.Min., is associate professor of pastoral theology and chair of the Department of Christian Ministries at Azusa Pacific University.

Keith H. Reeves, Ph.D., is professor of New Testament and early Christian literature at Azusa Pacific University.

Paul Shrier, Ph.D., is associate professor of practical theology at Azusa Pacific University.

Daniel Speak, Ph.D., is associate professor of philosophy at Azusa Pacific University.

Kenneth L. Waters Sr., Ph.D., is associate professor of New Testament at Azusa Pacific University.

Steve Wilkens, Ph.D., is professor of philosophy at Azusa Pacific University.

Gerald H. Wilson, Ph.D., is professor of Old Testament and biblical Hebrew at Azusa Pacific University.

William Yarchin, Ph.D., is associate dean and professor of biblical studies at Azusa Pacific University.